THE
LORE
of
WHISKY

THE
LORE
of
WHISKY
ALICE PARSONS

JCP

First published by
Jane Curry Publishing 2013
(Wentworth Concepts Pty Ltd)
PO Box 780 Edgecliff NSW 2027 Australia
www.janecurrypublishing.com.au

National Library of Australia Cataloguing-in-Publication entry

Author:	Parsons, Alice.
Title:	The Lore of Whisky/Alice Parsons
ISBN:	9781922190727 (hardback)
Notes:	Includes index.
Subjects:	Whisky.
	Whisky Scotland.
	Whisky Ireland.
	Whisky America.
	Whisky Australia.
	Whisky Tasmania.
	Whisky industry Tasmania.
	Distilleries Tasmania.

Dewey Number: 641.252

Cover and internal design: Cheryl Collins Design
Printed in China

I dedicate this book
to my very dear parents
M and D.

CONTENTS

Foreword by Bill Lark
aka The Godfather of Australian Whisky

The Lore of Whisky has arrived at a time when the world of whisky is opening up to countless new enthusiasts. Around the globe people are discovering how much enjoyment can be found in sharing the appreciation of malt whisky with friends.

A worldwide glut of Scotch whisky occurred when Glenfiddich found itself burdened with excess malt whisky in the 60s and 70s, ushering in a new era of whisky appreciation. Up until this time malt whisky had primarily been applied to grain spirit to produce Scotch Blends, and was not readily available to the wider market.

Whisky books written at that time concentrated on providing very technical and detailed accounts of every single distillery, and every whisky produced in the UK. For the whisky tragic these were bibles, the sole means by which to enter the fascinating world of malt whisky appreciation.

Since then the whisky industry and in particular 'malt whisky indulgence' has grown. It has become a destination for some, while for others it is perhaps the beginning of an adventurous journey. Enthusiasts now aim to be armed with an informative collection of facts and anecdotes, so that they may hold their heads up high in any whisky company around the world.

The Lore of Whisky delivers this in spades, or should I say tumblers. It is such an enjoyable and enlightening read on all matters whisky. As a malt whisky distiller, and probably a whisky tragic, certainly a whisky consumer, I give thanks to Alice for opening the door to many new friends and making them feel at home.

Introduction

George Bernard Shaw described whisky as liquid sunshine, and he was absolutely right. For me a glass of whisky is like a sunlit oasis, consistently full of promise. Whisky the subject glows brightly too, and whisky the story never slows.

> *The proper drinking of Scotch whisky is more than just indulgence: it is a toast to civilization, a tribute to the continuity of culture, a manifesto of man's determination to use the resources of nature to refresh mind and body and enjoy to the full the senses with which he has been endowed.*[1]

Writing this book has been one of my life's most exhilarating experiences. I have made new friends over whisky and had endless fascinating conversations surrounding it. There is a malty magic to whisky and I am utterly spellbound. As I face my publisher's deadline I am still euphoric, still frantically trying to squeeze in more stories and facts. I do not want the dialogue to end. Luckily because the topic is whisky I imagine it never will.

I have followed blogs on whisky on the Internet; I have been lent a library of whisky books; I have listened to whisky lectures, whisky lullabies and whisky news bulletins being streamed live on-line; I have joined a number of virtual whisky associations; I even have whisky friends on twitter; and I have only just fallen short of writing my own whisky blog. I may have become a whisky tragic.

Whatever my fate, here follows a wonderfully articulated view of the spirit that in my mind truly captures the essence of everything *whisky*:

'The Whiskey Speech' addressed by a Mississippi state senator to the legislature in 1958:

If you mean whiskey, the devil's brew, the poison scourge, the bloody monster that defiles innocence, dethrones reason, destroys the home, creates misery and poverty, yea, literally takes the bread from the mouths of little children; if you mean that evil drink that topples Christian men and women from the pinnacles of righteous and gracious living into the bottomless pit of degradations, shame, despair helplessness, and hopelessness, then, my friend, I am opposed to it with every fiber [sic] of my being.

However, if by Whiskey, you mean the oil of conversation, the philosophic wine, the elixir of life, the ale that is consumed when good fellows get together, that puts a song in their hearts and warm glow of contentment in their eyes; if you mean Christmas cheer, the stimulating sip that puts a little spring in the step of a rich elderly gentleman on a frosty morning; if you mean that drink that enables man to magnify his joy and to forget life's great tragedies and heartbreaks and sorrow; if you mean that drink the sale of which pours into our treasuries untold millions of dollars each year, that provides tender care for our little crippled children, our blind, deaf, our dumb, our pitifully aged and infirm, to build the finest highways, hospitals, universities, and community colleges in the nation, then my friend, I am absolutely, unequivocally in favor [sic] of it. This is my position, and as always, I refuse to be moved on matters of principle.

My great grandmother was an author and her personal motto
was *Sto et stabo*.
Strong and upright.
This is how I like to think of a good bottle of whisky.
Sto et stabo

Thank you.

Alice Parsons
April 2013

**Wherever I explore Irish or American whiskey, I spell the spirit in the
way those countrymen do, out of deference to my Irish and American
ancestors. Otherwise I spell whisky in the manner of Scotland and
as we do here in Australia.**

Chapter 1

Lively Water

Etymology fascinates me: words, their sounds and their look. I am at home with the romance languages, but not being a native Gaelic speaker I would be delighted to manage the pronunciation of the two beautiful words, *uisce* or *uisge* with appropriate 'swish' and 'élan'. These are the early fifteenth century Gaelic words for water. From these evolved the compounds *uisce beatha* (Irish) and *uisge beatha* (Scottish) meaning 'distilled water'. Both have their origins in the Latin *aqua vitae* or 'water of life'; a term with which we are all familiar. Another translation of the Latin, my preferred translation, is the more evocative, 'lively water'. Other early translations of *aqua vitae* were *usque baugh*, *uskbeaghe*, *usquebath* and *usquebae*, but all you need is to hear the lyricism in *uisce*, (later whisky of course) and you are on the same track as I am.

Usquebaugh-baul

In 1703 Scottish writer, Martin Martin published *A Description of the Western Islands of Scotland* in which he refers to a whisky-like beverage made from oats and subsequently quadruple distilled which he named *usquebaugh-baul*:

> *Two spoonfuls of this Liquor is a Sufficient Dose; and if any Man exceed this, it would presently stop his breath, and endanger his life.*[2]

A few years ago, Mark Reynier and Jim McEwan of *Bruichladdich (Laddie) Distillery* on Islay set out to make their own fiery version of *usquebaugh-baul* and they succeeded. However, their zeal — not to mention the alcoholic percentage in their drink — had to be tempered eventually to a responsible (and palatable) strength of 63.5% ABV. (This was not before James May from the ubiquitous *Top Gear* program had used it to fuel a racing car!)

Poteen

With time other idiomatic words for whisky or brew emerged such as pep and poteen (also spelled poitin). Poteen is Irish for any illicit grog. (Scotch poteen was long ago known as peatreek.[3])

Enjoy these rousing excerpts from a typical nineteenth century Irish verse that demonstrates how poteen or 'lively water' might reliably and yet paradoxically enable you both to sink your sorrows and raise your spirits, take care of your blemishes, and provide you with an aphrodisiac!

> *So stick to the cratur'*[4] *the best thing in nature*
> *For sinking your sorrows and raising your joys*
> *Oh what moderation gives hope to a nation*
> *Or brings consolation like poteen me boys*
> *So stick to the cratur' the best thing in nature*

For sinking your sorrows and raising your joys
Oh what botheration, no dose in the nation
Can give consolation like poteen me boys.
So stick to the cratur' the best thing in nature
For sinking your sorrows and raising your joys
Oh since its perfection, no doctor's direction
Can cleanse the complexion like poteen me boys.
Then stick to the cratur' the best thing in nature
For sinking your sorrows and raising your joys
For there's nothing like whiskey to make maidens frisky
It soon separates all the men from the boys.

Al-k'ohl, its sources and its uses

Spirited *Homo sapiens*, being an inveterate party animal, has been brewing intoxicating refreshment for millennia wherever there was grain or another sugar yielding base available to ferment. Take grapes (wine), rice (saki) or molasses (rum) for example. The resulting liquid was then distilled (see Chapter Two) from whichever mash had been successfully fermented, to concentrate the desired alcohol. The distillations were not merely useful when entertaining; the Babylonians followed by the Egyptians and Chinese made use of concentrated alcohol in metal processing, and also in the production of perfumes and medication.

Al-k'ohl means 'essence' in Arabic. It is worth knowing that any essence emerging from the process of distillation is always colourless. If there is any colour, the liquor is not pure.

Early apparatus, the alembic still
One of the first detailed descriptions of distillation was written in the eighth century by an Arabic scholar, Jabir Ibn Hayyan (known in the West as Geber). He distilled spirit from heated wine, and in the process also produced the alembic still (in Arabic, *al-ambiq*). The apparatus consisted of a pot, where the wine was heated, connected to a condenser where the alcohol was collected after it had condensed and cooled.

The alembic still is generally referred to today as a pot still.[5] The other widely used alternative still is a 'continuous' or 'column' still, known also as a 'Coffey'. (More of which anon.)

> If the study of distilling through the ages whets your appetite, there is a very comprehensive work put out by a Dutch publisher, *The Art of Distillation* by R. J. Forbes in 1948, later republished in 1970.

Barley beer

There is little substantive written work about the evolution of whisky per se, although it is believed that distilling techniques successfully made their way to Ireland and then Scotland during the 1100s. Wine, widely used in distillation at this time in other countries was not easily cultivated in Ireland or Scotland, so 'barley beer', or *bere*, thought to have been brought to Scotland initially by the Vikings, became the drink of choice. It was distilled into a liquor that evolved over time to become whisky (*uisce* or *uisge*).

Irish Chieftain's heir succumbs to excess
In Ireland the first documented evidence that whisky, or similar, was being produced dates back to 1405 when it was recorded in *The Annals of the Kingdom of Ireland*,[6] the *Annals of Clonmacnoise*, that Richard

MacRaghnaill, son and heir to the Chieftain of Muintir-Eolais, died of a 'surfeit of drinking [*aqua vitae*]'. Sadly for poor MacRaghnaill, *aqua vitae* had become ironically *water of death*.

Burnt wine, or brandy

The word 'brandy' evolved from 'brandywine', or burnt wine, which evolved from the German *branntwein* (Dutch, *brandwign*), a drink of distilled wine. This, however, was not what was being drunk in Ireland.

The custom of distilling wine into deliciously intoxicating drinks became so popular that it grew a little out of hand, and so it was banned in Nuremburg in 1496.[7] The distillation of whisky has faced its own share of banning as will be seen.

400 bottles for King James IV

In Scotland meanwhile the earliest official record of whisky dates to 1494. The Scottish Exchequer Rolls of that year show that Friar John Cor procured eight bols of malt to make a*qua vitae* at Lindores Abbey in Fife, for his majesty, James IV (reigned 1488–1513). James was in residence at that time at his hunting lodge, Falkland Palace. (Eight bols of malt would amount to 580 kilograms, (1,120lbs), enough to make more than 400 bottles of today's whisky.)[8] This volume would have undoubtedly taken care of quite a number of festivities and social obligations.

To commemorate the event five hundred years later, one thousand four hundred and ninety-four numbered bottles of *Friar Cor Quincentenary* were produced by United Distillers. *Friar John Cor* is, they say, a dark, rich amber blended Scotch produced from ten different single malt whiskies including eighteen and twenty-six year old varieties representing all the different whisky regions in Scotland. Bottle No. 1 was delivered to Buckingham Palace. The Emperor of Japan, the then Chancellor Helmut Kohl and the then Prime Minister John Major numbered among other VIPs lucky enough to be issued with a bottle of this truly extraordinary whisky.

Spreading the word

The fact that it was a friar to whom malt was sent for the preparation of *aqua vitae* for His Majesty underpins the view that whisky production was a skill disseminated through Mediaeval Europe via its monks and monasteries. The apothecaries of the day also played a significant role. (See Chapter Nine) *Aqua vitae* was being produced primarily for medicinal purposes, for woes such as colic or smallpox.[9] This 'Renaissance-era' whisky was coarse, potent and raw-tasting, and probably not too kind on the liver. Nonetheless, it was hailed as a preserver-of-health and a cure-all elixir.

This premise was later utilised during Prohibition in America (1920–1933). Doctors realised they could make a few extra dollars handing out prescriptions of 'whiskey', for which permission was granted during the alcoholic strictures of that time. (See Chapter Eight)

Drinking vessels

One of the most significant distinctions between mediaeval *uisge* and the whisky that emerged later was that *uisge* or its equivalent was drunk directly after being distilled. That is, it was bottled without being aged. What makes whisky whisky, and today it is a matter of law (see Chapter Two), is its resting period or 'maturation' spent in oak.

The practice of storing *uisge* or grog in barrels was well underway by the 1700s. Scottish lairds had stores of empty port and sherry barrels that were perfectly suited to accommodating the increasing amount of *uisge* being produced. The less affluent used bottles and jugs which provided storage but none of the enrichment offered by the wooden barrels.

Whisky produced today

Dorling Kindersley's *Whisky Opus*[10] lists an astonishing number of countries and territories beyond those with which we are already familiar that are producing varieties of whisky, including the following: Australia (see Chapter Eleven) Liechtenstein and Pakistan, also Sweden, Spain, France, Belgium, The Netherlands, Germany, Austria, New Zealand, South Africa, India and Taiwan; not to mention Argentina, Brazil, Bulgaria, the Czech Republic, Denmark, Finland, Italy, Latvia, Poland, Turkey and more.

> *Antarctica is now the only continent on which the spirit [whisky] is not distilled.* [11]

Drinkers beware

However not all the whiskies produced in these places conform to even to the loosest of definitions of a whisky:

> *Any of several distilled liquors made from a fermented mash of cereal grains.*[12]

Whisky is in fact now sold, whether or not actually produced, in 200 markets around the world[13] and more 'domestic' whisky is made and drunk in India than there is Scotch whisky drunk in the entire world.[14]

Chapter 2

The nitty-gritty

Here follows a compendium of whisky notes for readers who are meeting whisky in all its guises for the first time. Some are critical to the understanding of whisky and some are possibly outside the core of essential learning, it depends simply on levels of curiosity. There is much terrain to cover with the lore, laws and fabric of the whisky business, but in my view it is only fitting to begin respectfully with Scotch whisky.

'Scotland is the undisputed whisky capital of the world, producing nearly two-thirds of the global supply.' [15]

The necessary technicalities

Scotch whisky is an entirely natural product made from barley/grain, water and yeast.[16] Geography, grain and water source, air, alcoholic content and quality all conspire together to define the extraordinary range of whiskies and whisky-related drinks with which we have the privilege of being acquainted today. So do the methods used in production, cask management and maturation.

> *Great fury, like great whisky, requires long fermentation.*
> (Truman Capote, 1924–1984)

Scotch whisky may only be designated as such if it has been distilled, matured and bottled in Scotland, and then only in oak casks with a capacity of no greater than 700 litres, (153 imperial gallons or 184 US gallons), for *no less than three years* with an ABV* of less than 94.8%, and which has a minimum ABV of 40%. It is only when those thirty-six months are up that the liquid in the barrels may be referred to as whisky. Until that point it may only be called spirit.

*Historically, the term 'alcohol proof' was used in Britain as a measurement of the alcohol (ethanol) content in an alcoholic drink; it was measured as 7/4 times the alcohol by volume (ABV). (A little hard for the mathematically challenged.) As time progressed, simple ABV took its place and is used today. However America continues to use the term 'proof' and this is defined as exactly twice the level of ABV. Thus, if a drink is 100 proof it is 50% alcohol or ABV. Simple once it's explained!

Whisky production

Whisky production is a highly technical procedure and I outline it as best and simply as I can.

Malting

First barley is soaked in warm water for a couple of days. This steeping softens it, causing it to start to germinate and release enzymes that convert its starch into fermentable sugars.

Germination

The soaking process is halted at this point, and the barley is dried out for about five days (depending on the climate). Traditionally each distillery would lay out their germinating barley on enormous malting floors inside the distillery where it would be 'ploughed'[17] back and forth by hearty malt men enabling air to get to every grain. The majority of Scottish distilleries now import pre-malted barley from specialist malt mills, such as *Port Ellen Maltings* on Islay. *Laphroaig* (Islay) and *Highland Park* (Orkney) are two exceptions. [18]

When the germination reaches a critical point the barley is dispatched to a kiln for drying. In many cases, some level of smoke from a peat-heated fire is introduced to add to it that smoky aroma and flavour intrinsically associated with whisky.

Gristing and mashing-in

The now malted barley is then milled into coarse grist (of husks, grits and flour) which is 'mashed-in', or 'struck' into a stainless steel vat (a mash tun) of water at a temperature of about 60–65°C (140–149°F). The process of mashing-in allows the warm water to wake up those enzymes in the malt and convert the remaining starch into sugar.

Sparging

When the mashing-in process is complete, the sugar is separated from the barley grains in a process called sparging. Further courses of hot water will be run through the mash tun at 72° (161°F) and finally 80° (176°), producing a sugary solution called the wort (or worts[19]). The wort is drawn off into another drum, the 'underback', thence to the 'washback' (made either from stainless steel or Oregon pine) for the next step in the process — fermentation. The residual 'draff' in the mash tun is converted into pellets or cake for cattle feed. (There is no alcoholic content by this stage!)

Fermentation

Now yeast, critical to the process, is pitched into the wort, which ferments for up to three days and produces a weak and crude beer-like liquid of about 7–8% alcohol. This is known as the wash.[20] Finally, pure spirit known also as 'new make spirit' is evaporated from the wash leaving behind any solid residue.

For the curious, the science and equipment for distillation are as follows:

Distillation

Alcohol starts to boil at 78.3°C (172.9° F), whereas water boils at a temperature of 100°C (212°F). So, when the fermented liquid (the wash) is heated, an alcohol-rich percentage of it boils first. This is then condensed.

Copper stills[21] (like giant kettles) are suited perfectly to their role in distillation, as copper has properties that eliminate unwanted sulphides that the barley may have collected from soil. With the application of heat, the base of the [copper] wash still heats up and alcoholic vapour slowly commences its metamorphosis as conveyed here:

Up through a cone-shaped steeple, the shapes of which vary a great deal. (Tall stills for example will provide a light-bodied whisky as lighter alcohols rise higher.)

Along a still's narrow 'swan neck'.

Down through a gently descending pipe, known as a 'Lyne arm'.

The vapour is then cooled, becomes liquid and goes into a second still, the 'spirit still'.

At the first-stage distillation, the liquid distillate is referred to as the 'low wines' emerging at approximately 23–25% ABV. (What remains is called pot ale. [22]) The low wines are then redistilled from the spirit still, when they morph into what is called 'whisky spirit' or 'new make spirit'.[23]

Refinement and maturation

The middle cut, the 'heart of the run' is now separated from the 'fores', or 'foreshot', (the first portion) and the 'feints' (the last portion) — also known respectively as the heads and tails — of the distillation. In other words, the first portion and last portion of distillate are carefully monitored and specific quantities of both are extracted. This is because they may carry a distasteful metallic flavour you would not want in your whisky. The cutting and selection process is reliant absolutely on the skill and discernment of the distiller.

A far more succinct and user-friendly explanation of whisky production is:

We make beer and then we vaporise the alcohol, which we then condense to make whisky.[24]

The resulting spirit or 'heart' of the distillation is poured into oak barrels, or casks, which over time convert the spirit to whisky. (Most 'new make whisky' is diluted to about 63.4% ABV before it is placed in barrels for aging.)

Barrels

The role of the barrels is fundamental to the whole process of whisky production. Their properties directly affect the colour and flavour of the whisky being aged within them. Oak casks that have been used to age or 'mature' other spirits such as sherry or port (from Europe) or bourbon, (from America) are used. The former tends to produce a whisky of a darkish colour, with a longish finish [aftertaste], and the latter tends to produces whiskies that are more likely to be lighter with vanilla notes. Mark Reynier from *Bruichladdich* refers to the process of enhancing the flavours of whisky as 'taming' them.[25]

The Scotch whisky industry will re-use casks up to three or four times, depending on their condition, and the number of years they have been put to work maturing whiskies. (Up to about twenty years.) Casks being re-used are called 'refill casks' and the impact of the cask on the flavour and colour of a whisky during maturation understandably lessens each time it is used. In the aging of bourbon on the other hand, new casks are always used (see Chapter Seven). Also, whisky may be matured in more than one cask; for example, *The Balvenie 'Double Wood' Aged 12 Years* is aged first in oak 'for many years' to mellow it, and then in oak sherry casks for a few months, to bring a 'fruity honey depth to the whisky'.

The size of a barrel (or cask) is, give or take, 136 litres (36 gallons), and a hogshead 300 litres (54 gallons).

It interested me to learn that sugar density is measured by some whisky producers in degrees 'Plato'!

Chapter 3

Variations
on a theme

Malt: Noun. Barley or other grain that has been steeped, germinated, and dried, used for brewing or distilling, and making vinegar.[26]

Origin: Old English *m(e)alt*, of Germanic origin, related to *melt*.

Single malt whiskies

Single malt accounts for 10% of the Scotch whisky market.[27]

Single malt whiskies are double distilled in copper pot stills and aged in oak for a minimum of three years. However malts from *Auchentoshan* and *Hazelburn* are triple distilled. Single malts are premium products, made exclusively in any given single distillery in Scotland, and are made from a mash of only one grain — malted barley.

> *The single malts are more redolent of the true peaty whisky flavour than the normal brands of commerce, and cost more not only because they are longer matured — … — but are of normally higher strength.*[28]

Single malts have long been considered the epitome of everything that is glorious about whisky. (As cognac is to wine.) They purport to capture the essence of their specific origin. You may indeed be able to taste and savour the heather, the sea salt or the soft peat of their birthplace.

> *Whisky is a metaphor for the spirit and the soul of the people and the place where it is produced.*[29]

Recently I was introduced to *Laphroaig, Islay Single Malt Scotch Whisky* by a family friend, Randall, and for me this was ground breaking. The *Laphroaig* was rich, strong, delicious and invigorating. The smoky, peaty aftertaste embedded itself in my taste buds and remained immovable for at least a day, and after only one glass! I am now totally clear about the notes, 'smoky' and 'tobacco'. The bottle's label claims, that *Laphroaig* is 'The most richly flavoured of all Scotch whiskies', and I have no trouble believing it. Apparently it is sometimes compared to TCP, a European antiseptic![30] Others liken it to mouthwash. Iain Banks, author of *Raw Spirit* an absolutely wonderful book, describes *Laphroaig* very aptly as 'an extreme whisky'!

Malt does more than Milton can to justify God's ways to man.
(A.E. Housman, 1859–1936)

Single malt Scotch whisky brands are almost always named after the distillery in which they have been produced, for example, *Glen Moray Speyside Single Malt Scotch Whisky* (established 1897), whereas with blended Scotch whiskies this is not so. They may contain whisky from many distilleries. (Incidentally *Glen Moray* is aged in chardonnay casks; it is very mellow and one friend of mine, Mark, refers to it as a *breakfast whisky*!)

Judiciously blended and quietly married

The *Bailie Nicol Jarvie*, 'a blend of Old Scotch Whisky', is named after a person, the self same Bailie, famous for holding a wild sword-wielding highlander at bay, and rather than doing him untold harm with a red hot poker, which may have inflamed all sorts of drama, he avoided bloodshed by merely setting fire to his opponent's 'bonnie new plaid'. 'Aged with honour' as befitting its namesake, this finest of drinks is, 'carefully matured, judiciously blended and quietly married'. It is also perfectly delicious and boasts, according to its label, 'the highest malted content of any blended Scotch whisky'.

Only one single malt Scotch whisky distillery has been named after a person, rather than a place, that being the *Glen Grant Distillery* in Rothes in Speyside, founded in 1840, after Major James Grant.

Many other distilleries (and the single malts produced therein) retain their native Gaelic. Examples are: **Bunnahabhain** (1881) meaning 'mouth of the river' from Islay, and '**Cardhu**' (1824), meaning 'black rock' from Speyside.

Single malts have typically been associated with single malt Scotch, although they are now produced in many other countries: for example Japan (*Suntory*

Yamazaki Single Malt 12 Year Old Whisky), India (*Amrut Fusion*) and significantly in Australia such as *Lark's Cask Strength Single Malt Whisky 58%* ABV.

Glenfiddich, meaning 'glen, or valley, of the stag' pioneered single malt whisky, and today is the most awarded single malt in the world. (Incidentally *Glenfiddich* will not on-sell whisky to blenders, that is with the exception of Grant.)

- *Glenfiddich* (15% world market share in 2010)[27]
- *Glenlivet* (10.9%)
- *Macallan* (9.0%)
- *Glen Grant* (5.9%)
- *Glenmorangie* (4.8%)
- *Cardhu* (4.7%)
- *Abelour* (3.4%)
- *Laphroaig* (3.1%)
- *Balvenie* (2.6%)
- *Isle of Jura* (1.6%)

Japan and the largest malt distillery in the world

Japan is the second largest producer of single malt whisky after Scotland. Interestingly it is also home to the largest malt distillery in the world, The *Hakushu Distillery* owned by *Suntory*. Japan also produces single-grain whiskies. For example, *1984 Kawasaki Cask Strength Single Grain Japanese Whisky* and *Suntory Chita Single Grain Whisky.*

The Japanese whisky industry was developed in the 1920s. Its pioneers were Shinjiro Torii founder of *Suntory*, and Masataka, founder of *Nikka*. *Suntory* and *Nikka Distilleries*, along with *Kirin Distillery*, produce most of

Japan's whisky. The Japanese appear to have not confined their style to any particular formula. Besides the single malts and grains, they also make up blends of rye and barley. Further, they produce peated and unpeated whiskies, and mature them in a variety of casks.[32]

Grain whisky

Grain whisky is made from a mixture of malted and un-malted barley or other grains, such as wheat or maize, together with yeast or water, and then distilled in a Patent or Coffey (continuous distillation) still. This process generally produces a lighter spirit than the malts that are distilled in pot stills. Grain whisky is used chiefly in blending. An example is *Snow Grouse Blended Grain*, bottled by the company Official.

Blended malts

A blended malt is defined as a whisky made with single malts from more than one distillery. These contain no grain whisky, which is not the same as blended whisky, or blended Scotch whisky, as described below. They are aged a minimum of three years under the same laws as single malt Scotch whisky. An example is *Cutty Sark Blended Malt*.

Monkey Shoulder

Monkey Shoulder is a blend of three malts, *Glenfiddich*, *Balvenie* and *Kininvie* all from Speyside. The name derives from a malaise (today we would no doubt call it RSI or repeated stress injury) that literally struck at the bulky shoulders of the 'malt men' whose job it was to hand turn the barley for hours on end during malting process. (They continue in this task today.)

Nota Bene: a *pure malt* is not necessarily a *single malt*.

Blended whisky
Blended whisky on the other hand is a mixture of malt and grain whiskies from different distilleries. Typically a blend will include a much larger proportion of grain whisky than malt (70/30%) but different brands contain different proportions. (Sometimes use is made of de-flavoured spirit caramel to adjust the colour.). Examples of blended Scotch whisky are *J&B Rare*, *Famous Grouse*, *Grant's Famous Reserve*, *Bell's*, *Dewar's White Label*, *Haig Gold Label*, *Islay Mist* and *Vat 69*.

Many of the familiar great names in the larger family of the Scotch whisky business, Haig, Buchanan, Dewar, Walker, Grant, Sanderson, Teacher and Bell date back many generations. Some businesses are still managed by descendants of the founders who in their day most likely would have been farmers with a sideline knowledge in distilling.[33]

A whisky simply described as a Scotch, Irish, or Canadian whisky is often, though not necessarily, a blend.

Blending
The founding father of the Scottish whisky industry is considered to be Andrew Usher (1826–1898). He learned much from his father, also Andrew Usher (1782–1855), who perfected the art of blending whisky. They both saw that when grains were added to the coarse and bitter alcohol (*uisge*) of the day, it took on a much sweeter and mellower character.

In blending a skilled master blender, nosing or sniffing rather than tasting the separate components, mixes together spirits from different distilleries, from different casks, and likely of different ages* to ensure and maintain the taste and quality standards of a particular brand. This is a highly refined art. The olfactory prowess of the blender will be called into account as they may require more than 50 different ingredients to arrive at the delicate and perfect balance that is sought. And they must do this not just once, but time and time again. *J&B Rare* for example, nominated by IWSR (The International Wine and Spirit Research)[34] as the No. 1 whisky in Europe, and the No. 5 Scotch whisky in the world, is made up from no less than 42 whiskies.[35] Incidentally, most blended whiskies are bottled at 40% ABV.

Jim McEwan, distiller at *Bruichladdich* describes blends as providing the 'flight path' for the malt drinkers of the future.[36] They are an ideal starting point for whisky discovery, unlikely to be overwhelming (in the fashion say of a heavily peated malt) and therefore more likely to coax the protagonist-taster to venture further into the world of whisky.

The top ten Scotch whisky blended brands' world market shares are as follows:[37]

- *Johnnie Walker* (17.6%)
- *Ballantine*'s (6.6% — note the leap there)
- *J&B Rare* (6.3%)
- *Grant's* (5.5%)
- *Chivas Regal* (4.7%)
- *Dewar's* (4.0%)
- *Famous Grouse* (3.3%)
- *Bell's* (3.1%)
- *Label 5* (2.7%)
- *William Peel* (2.6%)

*Age statements

If the age of a blend or malt is noted on a whisky label, the age is that of the youngest whisky contained in the blend or malt and not an average age. The age statement on a label of Scotch whisky refers to the length of time the spirit has matured in the cask. This means that once the whisky emerges from the cask and is bottled, its age is fixed. The longer the time spent in the barrel however, the smoother the whisky promises to be. It reacts with the oak wood and the oxygen in the air, which over time render it softer and sweeter.

Historically, it was incontrovertibly maintained that the finest whisky needed to be aged for a minimum of ten years. Today however it is becoming clear that, by using smaller casks, extremely fine single malts may be produced that do not have an absolute need to rest ten years before being put on the market. The smaller cask means the spirit reacts more quickly and expediently with the wood, because of the greater ratio of exposure. Thus fewer and fewer age statements are being included on whisky labels today. They used to be a necessary boast but today revised aging methods have led to their decreased impact.

Even as methodology or so-called efficiency evolves, nothing can eclipse the thrill of meeting a bottle of whisky that may have rested for as much as thirty, let alone forty, fifty or sixty years.

Friendship is like whisky, the older, the better. ANON

Cask strength or barrel-proof whiskies

Cask strength or barrel-proof whiskies are rare, and usually only the very best whiskies are bottled in this way. They are bottled directly from the cask and undiluted, or only very slightly diluted. This, predictably, signifies that they will have a higher ABV. Examples are: Tasmania's *Sullivan's Cove Cask Strength Single Cask Malt Whisky* at 60% ABV, or *Overeem* (sherry cask matured) at 60% ABV. Whisky, as stated, is normally sold at 40% ABV but it does not start its life out like that. Generally it goes into the barrel at about 65% ABV and is cut back with water before bottling.

'Single cask' or 'single-barrel' whiskies

'Single cask' or 'single-barrel' whiskies are a special category of single malts, or single grains, and are generally bottled by specialist independent bottlers, for example Duncan Taylor, Gordon & MacPhail, or Kentucky Bourbon Distillers (in America). Each bottle of single-barrel whisky is, as the name suggests, from an individual cask. Bottles therefore are often labelled with specific barrel and bottle numbers, and significantly the taste may vary considerably from cask to cask within a brand. Examples I have sampled are *Balvenie 15 Year-Old Single Barrel Scotch Whisky* and *Rittenhouse Rye 25 Year-Old*. While diverse, both were memorably bracing experiences.

Independent bottlers and dead soldiers

Independent bottlers play a number of important roles in the world of whisky. They often rescue the casualties of the business, the distilleries that have for whatever reason had to close down [aka dead soldiers]. While their operations may be dead, their product, though orphaned, may not have expired. Barrels remain which are happily given a new life under the wing of independent bottlers. This also provides a source of revenue for distillers. The independents' innovations bring a new dimension to the marketplace. And they also provide a conduit to the public for those distillers who have single malts but do not incline to do their own bottling.

Meadowside Blending, based in Scotland, is an example of an independent bottler. They specialise in rare single malts and blends. Recently they released a *21 Year-Old Bowmore* from 1989 that has 'spent its life maturing in bourbon'.[38] It is released under Meadowlands' *Maltman* range and comes in at 46% ABV.

Gordon & MacPhail

This company was established in 1895. Today their warehouses contain probably the largest collection of matured malt whiskies in the world. This was a prerequisite for the 2010 release of the world's oldest single malt ever bottled: *70 Year Old Mortlach*.[39] This whisky was the first release in a new range called *Generations* and was followed in March 2011 by a *70 Year Old Glenlivet* together with another five bottlings of *Glenlivet* dating from the 1950s to 1980s. They also have a significant amount of *Macallan* dating back to 1940 that has led to the release of a special range from there, called *Speymalt*. *Gordon & MacPhail* also produce blended whiskies such as *Ben Alder*, *Glen Calder* and *Avonside*.

On an aeroplane I recently enjoyed some absolutely delicious *Glenlivet 12 Year Old*. I only wish the bottle had not been so woefully small! Next to me on the same plane was a delightful gentleman, John, who told me that back in the late 1960s he used to buy the finest *Macallan* from the Hole in the Wall pub at Waterloo Station for 2s9d. This came in at tuppence more than the ordinary blended whiskies being served for 2s7d!

Macallan 50 Year Old is, I recently noticed in the film *Skyfall*, 007's malt of choice.

Chapter 4

Scotland's whisky territories and other facets of the business

How best to store it? How long mature it? How to safeguard it and how to promise maximum return for your effort, and pleasure for your palate? The business of whisky is complex and challenging, never dull and critically never predictable. That is why it is such a thrilling enterprise and why it holds so many in its thrall. It is also why you may as well devote the rest of your life to exploring the infinite variety of whiskies and working out for yourself which has the essence that will speak to your soul.

Angel's share

The angel's share, also known as the angel's tax, is a mythical explanation for the way in which whisky casks can lose from between 2–3% of their volume every year. For myth-believers rather than misbelievers, this has nothing to do with evaporation, rather it is the angels drawing down their annual 'share' and generously ensuring that the whisky is entirely suitable for our consumption. Once bottled, the whisky is angel-secure.

Whiskies typically do lose alcohol strength as well as volume as they mature. With whiskies being aged for as much as thirty years, for example, attention has to be given to ensuring that the alcohol strength does not drop below the minimum permitted 40% ABV. And while distillers may lose more than 3–4% of the spirit to evaporation in the UK they will only be allowed a concession of 3% as far as the taxman is concerned. In Australia, a concession may be made up to 4–5%. It goes without saying that alcohol shrinkage is an expensive consideration in the production of whisky.

During maturation, periodic checks are run to establish the volume remaining in the cask, to test the alcoholic strength and to check colour and nose. While it might seem a splendid idea to check the taste of the whisky being matured in your casks, you would be ill advised to taste check them all in one go because of the predictable ill effects that might be occasioned.

Leakers and tappers

Besides evaporation, casks occasionally leak if their hoops have become loose, or their staves fractionally separated. This may occur because of shrinkage if a warehouse is very dry.

A traditional means of checking against any loss brought on in such a way is for the warehousemen to literally 'tap' the sides of the casks to ensure there is no ominous 'empty' echo sound.

A distillery's efficiency is measured by the yield achieved from a metric tonne of barley. Typically this volume produces 400 litres (88 imperial gallons, or 105 US gallons).

Charring

When a cask has done its dash a number of times it can be rejuvenated by the process of charring. The cask is scraped out mechanically to a 'new wood' condition. Then a gas flame is used to gently burn the fresh surface. The flame opens fissures in the wood that assist the maturation process. (Care is taken not to be too zealous, so as not to overwhelm the promised spirit with an excessively burnt or smoky flavour.) Charring can be effected on a barrel, or cask, several times, as there are only a couple of millimetres of the wood's surface removed at each session. Oak is a hard wood and so not deeply impregnated by the spirit. Charring caramelises the sugars in the timber and these help filter out any impurities in the new spirit that take up residence there.

American oak is used extensively in the manufacture of sherry casks, which are used multiple times (they can have a life span of up to about 20 years); but when aging bourbon, since Prohibition it has been a matter of law, that casks may only be used once. This was more to do with the Coopers' Union than the distillers. Allowing their casks multiple uses did not promise prosperity, so it was decided that there would be only one cask per distillation.

Scotland's whisky territories

The six single malt regions of Scotland are the Lowlands, the Highlands, Speyside, Islay, Campbeltown and the Islands.

The terrain in the Lowlands is one of gently rolling hills, and it is not surprising that the whisky from here reflects this, being typically soft and light with malty, grassy characteristics. Its aromas are similarly subtle and delicate. There are very few distilleries still in operation in the Lowlands. However, examples include *Glenkinchie* near Edinburgh, known too as The *Edinburgh Malt* (and which can boast the largest wash still in Scotland), *Blandoch*, down in the Borders, and *Auchentoshan* near Glasgow. A tasting note for the Lowlands would typically suggest the following:

Light, vanilla, leafy, malty and fruity.[40]

The Highland region offers the greatest variety of malts. This is because it is a large and more diverse region with tall mountains divided by deep glens, lochs and broad valleys. It covers the area north of an imaginary line between North Glasgow on the West and North Edinburgh on the East. It excludes Speyside, which constitutes its own sub-region, (see below). Excuse the pun, but it would be fruitless to make sweeping generalisations about the whisky produced in the Highlands (and no definitive generalisations can be made about any of the regions), although in the Highlands you can expect spicy, lightly peated, citrus, and floral aromas.[41] The region produces whiskies that range from dry to sweet. Some have stirrings of smoke and peat. Examples from the heart of the Highlands are *Dalwhinnie*, *Glengoyne* and *Edradour* and, from further north, *Old Pulteney* and *Glenmorangie* (the biggest selling whisky in Scotland and to date my favourite.)

Speyside lies within the Highland region and encompasses the Spey valley, by the River Spey. It is here that almost half of Scotland's malt whisky distilleries are to be found, about 50 to be closer to the mark. This small area of land to the northwest of Aberdeen is lush and fertile and typically produces mellow, sweet, floral, grassy and particularly fruity malt whiskies.[42] Some of the best-known examples from here are *Glenfiddich*, *Glenlive*t and *Macallan*.

The island of Islay (pronounced I-la) is the southern most island of the lower Inner Hebrides and has often been called 'The Queen of the Hebrides' as well as 'Whisky Island'. The making of whisky is integral to the place itself. It is home to no fewer than eight working distilleries and has a population of only 3,500. Its total land mass is 600 square kilometres (231 square miles) of which at least a quarter is covered in peat. Burning peat was once Islay's main fuel source and now it is the signature flavour of Islay whisky. Examples include *Bruichladdich, Lagavulin, Caol Ila, Bowmore, Ardbeg** and *Laphroaig*. According to a report from 1863[43] Glasgow taverns were known to divide their whisky into four categories of ascending quality: middling, good, Islay and undiluted Islay.

*Legend relates that Celtic monks used to find safe haven on Islay when being persecuted by raiding Norsemen. They smuggled their precious 'aqua vitae' into the rocky (still extant) cove at Ardbeg.

Ardbeg was officially established as early as 1815 but was closed in 1983. Happily Glenmorangie PLC (under the parent company of LVMH or Louis Vuitton Moët Hennessy) came to the rescue, and bought the distillery in 1997. The purchase and restoration of the distillery cost a rumoured $14.5M AUD (£10M GBP).

Campbeltown, the fifth region, once upon a time boasted 30 distilleries but now there are just three: *Springbank*, *Glengyle* and *Glen Scotia*. Campbeltown's whiskies tend to have a little peat and salt, and generally are medium to full-bodied. A tasting note might also contain terms such as malty, nutmeg, fruity and light smoke.[44] Three examples (all single malts) are *Hazelburn*, *Springbank* and *Longrow*.

The sixth region comprises 'The Islands': Arran, Jura, Mull, Orkney, Skye and Lewis with their respective distilleries: *Arran*, *Isle of Jura*, *Tobermory*, *Highland Park* and *Scapa* (founded in 1885 — its single malt is *Scapa Single Orkney Malt* — a great name), *Talisker* (the only distillery on Skye) and *Abhhain Dearg*.

🪶 **There are approximately 98 distilleries in operation in Scotland at the time of writing.**[45]

The Scotch Whisky Industry Review produced by the leading Scotch whisky analyst, Alan S. Gray, is the definitive information source for all Scotch whisky says Alan Gordon, whose own *Essential Guide to Whisky* has been an invaluable resource for me in my whisky odyssey. Some of Gray's statistics follow here. (The current edition of *The Scotch Whisky Industry Review* is available for £475.)

In 2005, the estimated worldwide consumption of Scotch whisky was approximately 300 million litres, (800,000 gallons), and the top export market by volume was France, and by value, the United States of America. France remains the top export market today.[46]

Chapter 5

Whisky-related etiquette and related syndromes

If man should find the perfect amount
of whisky to drink each day he will live forever.[47]

Tasting

The routine is like a slow four-step. That is: sip, savour, swill and swallow (all the while remembering to breathe). This routine offers firstly the *initial impression* and taste sensation, then the *mouthfeel** and the *expansion of flavour* as you taste and swallow. Then you progress to the very significant *finish* and the lingering *aftertaste*.

When tasting malt whiskies, the glass should be tulip-shaped. Contrary to what might be expected, the cut glass whisky tumbler is not suited to the purpose. The tulip shape concentrates the bouquet, the volatile aromas and the colour.

I have learned a lot about nosing from watching Scottish Master Blender Richard Paterson on the screen, and more locally through Larry Aronson at World of Whisky[48] in Sydney and Mark Nicholson at *Lark Distillery*[49] in Hobart, Tasmania. Richard Paterson's guidelines are as follows. Firstly you hold the tasting glass by its stem and never the bowl like you might a brandy balloon, or tumbler. Then, when nosing, you put your nose forward into the glass, not just once but *four* times. Richard makes great theatre out of the moment but whisky is ideally suited to be enjoyed theatrically from time to time.

He suggests that you say to your whisky, 'Hello' and then withdraw your nose for a second, and then you pop (or plunge) your nose back into the heart of the glass and say, 'How are you?' and then your inner monologue might continue: 'Quite well' … 'Thank you'. He also recommends that once you are at the tasting stage of the ritual, you swill the whisky in and around your tongue for the number of seconds that equate to the age of the whisky. (Quite hard work if it is a 30 year-old!) Ian Buxton[50] describes this motion as 'chewing'.

As important as is the nose in this exercise, so is an uncompromised palate. No garlic bread at lunch or spicy curries for nosers and tasters of whisky. Further, according to instructions from The Scotch Malt Whisky Society,

> ...water is essential in tasting full-strength malts. Not only does it soften the influence of the alcohol, it draws out the nose of the whisky to an astonishing extent. In nosing try to divest yourself of expectation and concentrate on the present experience.[51]

It is critical in all matters where water and whisky meet that the water be as pure as is possible.

The mouthfeel

The mouthfeel is significant for whisky lovers but absolutely critical to distillers when cutting into the heart of a spirit when it is going through the distillation process. The mouthfeel of a spirit enables the distiller to discern when the initial oily or bitter 'fores' yield to the clear and desired spirit. At the end of the process the mouthfeel alerts them to the distasteful presence of the 'feints' in the liquor prompting them to cut the spirit at that point.

Whisky tastes and nose power

The primary tastes are four: sweet, sour/acidic, salty, and bitter/dry, while the primary aromas are 23! According to the tasting notes from the Scotch Malt Whisky Society, the nose can pick up scents diluted to one part in a million; the nose, (your and my nose, too) is a seriously sophisticated piece of equipment.

As the eye, yours and mine, has such a will of its own, leaping to conclusions because of colour and prefixed notions, expert nosers and professional tasters sometimes make use of cobalt blue glasses to protect them from themselves. If you are casting an eye over whisky and are not wearing cobalt blue glasses, the colour of a malt may give an indication of its character, but colour evaluations can be unreliable.

There are traditionally held to be seven main scent groups: esters, phenols, aldehydes, sweet-associated, cereals, oils and woods. Then there are multiple combinations of these, thus malt whisky tasting is so challenging (and thrilling).

Esters:	fruit, flowers, pear drops
Phenols:	medicinal, peaty, smoky
Aldehydes:	hay, grass, leather
Sweet-associated:	vanilla, toffee, honey
Cereals:	malt, bread, wheat
Oils:	butter, hazels, walnuts
Woods:	cedar, patch-pine, resin

Incidentally, the peatiness of malt is measured by the parts per million (p.p.m) of the aromatic phenol it contains.

Whisky jargon
Your whisky may have any of the following attributes:

Its nose may be like old worn saddle leather, chewed tobacco spit or a hint of dark chocolate; or it might be as though wrapped in waxy dark chocolate. Alternatively it could be fruity, floral, spicy or smoky. Or it may be peaty or peaty 'infused with zesty lemon and lime'. It could bring to mind black pepper, smoked fish, crispy bacon or bold menthol, green capsicum (peppers), or briny sea spray on chalky cliffs. Another might evoke waxed lemon, coal tar soap, beeswax camphor, toasted vanilla, sizzling cinnamon, warm hazelnut, almond toffee, ripe bananas, creamy cappuccino or espresso coffee, toasted marshmallow or even, spicy plum pudding, dusty hessian bag, burnt rubber, or liquorice!

Here is a great definition of *Ancient Age 10 Star*:

> *It is clean, sharp and minty and it laughs at ice.*[52]

The matter of ice

I fully appreciate that for many the addition of ice to whisky is considered wanton and barbaric, but for the heathen who may want a whisky-cooling-aid, here is an ideal way of keeping whisky cool for a goodly stretch of time: Japanese ice balls. These are a bit of fun. Owing to the name, I can only assume that a Japanese came up with the concept.

Further to research, I can offer up two pieces of advice on how to conjure these 'ice balls'. One is to employ your own personal Japanese sculptor who will fashion you your ice balls at whatever the going rate may be. Alternatively and much more simply, go and buy yourself some party balloons, fill them with distilled water (or from where I am sitting, pure rain water) to a volume that will best suit your preferred whisky tumbler (and be generous), and then rest the filled balloons in an appropriate vantage point in your freezer until they have frozen solid. Finally take a pair of scissors, cut of the top of the balloon and peel away the balloon 'skin' exposing your ice ball all ready to be of service.

It has been pointed out to me that one of the dangers of putting ice cubes in your whisky is that the whisky will be bound to absorb the taste of the ice which is bound to have absorbed the flavour of anything that happened to be in your freezer the day you froze it. If you use pure water and incubate it in a balloon, this no longer need be a concern. (And for the cynical, no, there is no aftertaste of rubber in this process.)

The Scots did originally use pebbles and stones from seashore, loch or riverbank in order to chill their whisky, rinsed of course! Thus evolved the usage and expression, 'on the rocks'. Obviously you could follow the old practice, or with a bit of luck find a commercial version of them in your local whisky store or wine merchant's. They are widely marketed these days.

'Hair of the dog' for the compulsively convivial

In 1966 John Doxat, on behalf of Booth's, the prestigious London Distillery (dating back to the 1740s), put out an anthology of: 'Recipes, both simple and prodigious, collated to appeal to modern Taste …' There is a wealth of fabulous information in his anthology, however for now I just want to note Mr. Doxat's comments on the hair of the dog provided for those he describes as 'compulsively convivial'.

His advice ran as follows: That before an evening when the convivially addicted might want to forearm themselves, they could imbibe on some creamy milk or olive oil, 'or on a preliminary snack of sardines on buttered toast'. He posits that the ancient Romans, if bitten by a dog, would, in order to ward off any ill-effect, drink a potion containing burnt hair 'from that canine'. He observes that adding alcohol to a body already suffering from an excess of alcohol cannot do any good, medically speaking, although it may provide a temporary feeling of relief. With this I concur. He continues:

A universally esteemed cure is a pint of champagne….
This produces an [sic] euphoria which may pass for health;
and a desire for a further bottle.

Importantly here is a hangover remedy he provides which is more germane to our topic.

'HAIR OF THE DOG' COCKTAIL
Serves: 1

Ingredients:
30ml (1oz) Scotch
45ml (1½oz) heavy cream
15ml (½oz) honey

Method:
Shake vigorously (if you can stand the noise) with shaved ice, and strain into a cocktail glass.

The Quaich
Any story about whisky would be incomplete without a mention of the *quaich*.

When I purchased a pair of *quaich* in the London Silver Vaults sometime last century, I had no concept of their rich history. To me their petite size and balanced proportions were enough to convince me to buy them. (For anyone who has not seen one, they are shallow drinking bowls approximately 19cm (3½") across with a depth of about 2½cm (1") with two little handles at 9 o'clock and 3 o'clock.)

They are quaint and whimsical, and are perfect for storing trinkets such as rings or cufflinks. One of ours survived; the other I can only guess was equally appealing to some adolescent enjoying the hospitality of one of our teenaged children; being just the right shape not only for trinkets, but also for ashing cigarettes — whoosh! There one minute, gone the next.

The origin of the word *quaich*, or *quaigh*, comes from middle sixteenth century Scottish Gaelic, *cuach* or 'cup'. The two handles enabled simple tasting for clansmen as the *quaich* would be passed handle–to–handle, man–to–man about the fire, as stories were told and traditions entrenched. Today rare examples of three- and four-handled *quaich* may be found (sadly I have never seen one). Put simply, they are a delight to behold and designed absolutely for sharing, whether between lovers, friends or kinsmen.

They were originally made from carefully carved wood, probably imitating the form of a scallop shell from which distilled whisky was most likely drunk, and later in stone, brass, pewter and horn. Some were made with glass bottoms through which one could spy on one's fellow drinkers. Also there were *quaich* with bases of not one, but two plates of glass, in between which one might place a lock of hair of one's beloved, in the style of a locket (but much more fun).

Naturally there are some wonderful legends associated with these charismatic, little dishes. Apparently King James VI Scotland gave one as a wedding gift to his bride, Anne of Denmark, in 1589 when she was the tender age of fourteen; Bonny Prince Charlie (1720–1788) was known to keep one in his canteen, and Sir Walter Scot (1771–1832) apparently measured his drams in one.

Keepers of the Quaich

The charter of this exclusive non-profit society, formed by Scotland's whisky distillers in 1988, is to advance the industry and raise funds for charitable causes in Scotland. Membership is by invitation only, and is strictly limited to individuals who have the distinction of having made a significant contribution to the Scotch whisky industry. There are over 1,900 members from no less than 84 countries. A Keeper of the Quaich mentioned a number of times in this book is Ian Buxton, author of *101 Whiskies to Try Before You Die*. He is a Liveryman of the Worshipful Company of Distillers and a Grand Ordinary Member of the Von Poser Society. (The latter sounds intriguing.)

The Centenary Quaich

This trophy is presented to the winning team of Scotland's annual match with Ireland in Rugby Union's Six Nations tournament.

Chapter 6

Ireland

Traditionally the Irish make single malts such as *Bushmills Single Malt*, mentioned above, but also fine blends like *Jameson*. Neutral grains, such as wheat and oats, may be put in the mix to make it smoother. Irish whiskey is usually triple-distilled so is viewed by some as being purer than its Scottish counterpart. It is always aged a minimum of three years. Its smooth and soft characteristics make it very easy to drink. (I have been practising.) An example is *Redbreast 15 Year Old.* This is triple distilled in a single pot still. Another Irish distinction is that with the exception of *Connemara Peated Single Malt Irish Whiskey*, the Irish do not use peat in distilling.

The Irish sort [of whiskey] is particularly distinguished for its pleasant and mild flavour. (Dr Samuel Johnson, 1709–1784)

It was Aeneas Coffey, an Irishman, who invented a still (1831) that was more economical and simpler to use than the traditional pot stills (alembic). However, the Irish were reluctant to use it as they feared the whiskey it produced was inferior to what they were used to, and they were not enthusiastic about blending, a concept to which the Scots were more amenable. While Ireland was prolific in its production of whiskey in the nineteenth century,[53] historically there had been tens of hundreds of Irish distilleries,[54] their hesitancy gave Scotland the whisky edge. Ireland's poor relationship with England at this time did little to help their cause, and predictably their trade reduced quite dramatically and swiftly. Today there remain only three legal distilleries:

• *Bushmills Distillery* in County Antrim, Ireland's oldest, having been first granted a license to distil whiskey in 1608. *Bushmills Single Malt* is mellow and delicious.

• *Midleton* (dating back to 1795) in County Cork, which is where *The Irishman Original Clan Whiskey* is produced, and the much-celebrated *Jameson* for which I have a very soft spot.

Bushmills and *Midleton* are part of the Irish Distillers Group, whose parent company was Pernod Ricard but is now Diageo plc. (See Chapter Ten.)

• *Cooley Distillery* (built in 1987) in County Louth remains independent. It produces single grains and single malts and examples are: *Knappoque*, *Clontarf* and *Brennans*.

As with Scotch (for example Chivas Regal) or Canadian (Canadian Club) whiskey blends, Irish whiskey blends may be made up from different distilleries, so will not carry the name of a specific distillery. Jameson Irish Whiskey is an exception, as it is distilled in the distillery of its name.

IRISH COFFEE

A warm nostalgic fug overtakes me when I think of this heavenly brew.
Serves: 1

Ingredients:
60ml (2oz) Irish whiskey
150–180ml (5–6oz) strong, hot coffee
Quantity thick pouring cream
Sugar (optional)

Method:
Warm your toddy glass or goblet with hot water then drain.
Put whiskey into glass (with sugar if desired).
Pour in coffee and stir.
Pour in thick cream, preferably over the back of a spoon, so it floats seductively
on the surface.

IRISH GINGER TODDY

A top remedy for almost any ailment.
Serves: 1

Ingredients:
1tbs honey
Hot water
60ml (2oz) Irish whiskey
60ml (2oz) squeezed lemon juice
60ml (2oz) ginger beer
Cinnamon stick, or grated cinnamon for garnish

Method:
Put honey into a pre-heated coffee mug or latte glass.
Add a couple of tablespoons of hot water to dissolve it.
Add whiskey, lemon juice, ginger beer. Pour hot water to the top and stir.
Garnish with fresh ground cinnamon and serve.

Wakes and whiskey

> *Give an Irishman lager for a month, and he's a dead man. An Irishman is lined with copper, and the beer corrodes it. But whiskey polishes the copper and is the saving of him.* (Mark Twain 1835–1910)

I have no wish to be morbid but I felt the inclusion of an Irish custom that dates back millennia might find an appropriate spot right here. Most of us have been witness to an Irish wake either directly or through the medium of literature, television or cinema, and we are thus aware of how they are characterised by passion and sometimes high jinks, but always the odd dram of whiskey.

Wakes the style of which are observed in Ireland (or were until the 1970s except for some very rare and remote country districts today) date back to pagan times although they have become interwoven with Christian practices. What occasions they must have been, wrought with sadness yet buoyed by the heart and spirit of family and friends, and that other main player, whiskey.

The order of events and attendant rules at these highly traditional wakes were very clearly defined. Briefly, the corpse was bathed and laid out on a prepared bed or table in the parlour or main room, covered in white linen decorated with white or black ribbons and, if a child, flowers. A crucifix would be placed on the chest of the corpse and rosary beads threaded through the fingers. Candles were lit all about the body and clay pipes, tobacco and snuff placed throughout the room.

All male callers coming to pay their respects were bidden to take a puff on a pipe; the smoke would ward off evil spirits and possibly any unpleasant …

Clocks were stopped and mirrors turned around or covered, as a mark of respect, and the corpse was not for a moment to be left alone. Keening and wailing followed, demonstrating the depth of sorrow being experienced by the family, all led by the '*Caointhe*' (lead keener). Poetry was recited and lamentations cried out.

In the background meanwhile supplies were being gathered: bread, meat and all sorts of goodies, but most significantly whiskey. The whiskey was either whiskey itself, or a variation of it, 'poteen', a highly illegal and gloriously potent home-distilled brew. Wakes lasted for a number of days and nights; energy was to be sustained and respect paid in full.

Emotions would run in every direction as the wake proceeded; laughter and games were played as much to celebrate as to keep everyone awake. Those less energetic would sit around the kitchen table sipping tea laden with poteen or whiskey, exercising their minds rather than their limbs. It was all colour, motion and emotion, right through the night(s) until the day of the funeral.

On that day the body would be placed in an open coffin and taken outside where it would bide a while so all the mourners could make their farewells with a kiss. The coffin would then be closed and carried by four of the deceased's closest relatives, taking turns with other groups of four until they reached the graveyard. The coffin would duly be lowered into the ground, covered with soil and finally a shovel and spade in the shape of a cross would be laid across the site. Then I imagine a few whiskey nightcaps before a long deserved sleep.

Drown in a cold vat of whiskey? Death, where is thy sting?
(W.C. Fields, 1880–1946)

Chapter 7

America: whiskey categories and inviolable federal regulations

The true pioneer of civilization is not the newspaper, not religion, not the railroad — but whiskey! (Mark Twain, 1835–1910)

Straight: Once aged for two years a whiskey is entitled to call itself 'straight'. For example 'straight rye whiskey', provided it is made with a minimum of 51% of that specific primary grain, in this instance 'rye'. (If the whiskey produced contains less than 51% of a nominated grain, it may still be designated as 'straight', just a non-specific 'straight' provided it has been aged for those requisite two years.) About half the whiskey consumed in the USA is straight whiskey. *Whistle Pig Rye 10 Year Old* is an example of a top shelf straight rye whiskey.

By US Federal law, the following types of whiskey must be distilled to no more than 80% ABV or 160 proof, and no colouring or flavouring is allowed. Additionally they must be aged in new charred oak containers.

• Bourbon whiskey (its mash containing at least 51% corn or maize)
• Malt whiskey (its mash containing at least 51% malted barley)
• Rye whiskey (its mash containing at least 51% rye)
• Rye malt whiskey (its mash containing at least 51% malted rye)
• Wheat whiskey (its mash containing at least 51% wheat)

Corn whiskey (as opposed to bourbon whiskey, although confusingly bourbon in its early years was also referred to as corn whiskey) need not be aged. If it is to be, it is usually only aged for six months and, by regulation, in un-charred oak barrels, or in used barrels. (Often these are bourbon barrels.) Corn whiskey's mash must contain at least 80% corn.

These restrictions do not exist for some similarly named products in other countries, such as Canada. Corn is the most usual basis for the mash from which Canadian whiskey is distilled but rye, wheat and barley malt are also used. Canadian whiskey is aged for a minimum of three years in charred wooden casks and then blended to produce the delicately flavoured and light-bodied characteristics that are its widely recognised features. Canadian whiskey has to be produced and aged in Canada — just as Scotch whisky must be produced and aged in Scotland. The terms Canadian whiskey and Canadian rye whiskey are legally indistinguishable. Today the most popular Canadian whiskies are *Crown Royal*, *Canadian Club*, *Seagram's V.O.* and *Black Velvet*.[55]

Bottled-in-bond: While straight whiskey (or indeed any US spirit) is being aged, it is not liable to taxation. However, 'The Bottled Bond Act' of 1897, declared that any spirit had to be bottled and stored for at least four years (although longer is permissible) to ensure it was inherently of good value. It is to be bottled at a minimum of 100 proof (50% ABV) and placed in a 'bonded warehouse' tracked all the while by the Internal Revenue Service. Taxes only become payable when the whiskey or other liquor is released from the holding warehouse.

To be entitled to the label 'bottled-in-bond', the liquor has to be distilled during one distillation season, by one distiller in one distillery. The bottled product must then clearly state where the contents were distilled and, if bottled at a different location, this must be clearly noted too.

Light: This classification was established in 1972.[56] This whiskey is stored in standard or un-charred new oak containers and is between 161 and 189 proof. Blended light whiskey is mixed with less than 20% straight whiskey, and is made with corn. At an ABV of over 80% light is obviously a colour reference not content!

Rye whiskey, or 'rye' in the eastern United States is often synonymous with whiskey, even if it does not have a rye base, just as bourbon may also used conversationally for whiskey in the South and West. And on the subject of rye, can there be anyone out there whose toes can resist tapping to the ever-captivating melody and lyrics of Don McLean:

So bye, bye, Miss American Pie; Drove my Chevy to the levée but the levée was dry. Them good old boys was drinkin' whiskey and rye, singin' 'this'll be the day that I die'.

Bourbon

Bourbon, the Crown Prince, if not the King of American Whiskey, is after rum, America's native brew. Today bourbon makes up 35% of all spirits currently sold in the US. It is made with at least 51% corn or maize. The rest can be a mixture of grains, usually malted barley and rye, and sometimes wheat. In 1964 Congress, wishing to protect bourbon's name, declared that it was to be recorded as 'a distinctive product of the United States'. The very best would be 'bottled in bond' and aged at least four years in wood'.

 An un-aged bourbon may be called a *baby bourbon* while an un-aged whiskey may be called a *white whiskey*, or formerly a *white dog*!

Bourbon varies on average between 80 and 125 proof. This is equivalent of 40% ABV and 62.5% ABV. (The legal minimum is 60 proof or 30% ABV, this is 10% less than the minimum for Scotch whisky). The alcohol content may only be reduced by the use of iron-free limestone-filtered spring water. And while bourbon may be made anywhere, the only state that can legally put its name on the label, as a 'bourbon' product is Kentucky, as explained below. (*Wild Turkey* is a Kentucky Straight Bourbon Whiskey.) Nearly 80% of the world's supply of bourbon is indeed made in Kentucky in thirteen distilleries there. Most of the rest is made in Tennessee, Virginia, Missouri, California, Georgia, Illinois, Indiana, Ohio, and Pennsylvania.

 Should you want to develop a blended bourbon, your product must contain at least 51% straight bourbon.

Corn

Corn became the main player in the creation of bourbon when Scottish and Irish settlers made tracks towards the South and West US, notably after the conclusion of the Whiskey Rebellion in 1794. (See Chapter Eight). While expertly equipped with the skills of distilling, these newcomers could not lay their hands on the requisite quantity of grains such as the rye and barley with which to make grog or whiskey. Corn was indigenous and abundant, so the migrant farmers started brewing with it. This corn gave rise to bourbon, pioneered in Bourbon County, Virginia. (Bourbon County is now of course in Kentucky, further to the redefining of borders; hence Kentucky Bourbon.)

Kentucky Bourbon in its early years was served solely from barrels and only bottled from the 1870s onwards. However, it was being advertised fifty years earlier. The first advertisement for bourbon whiskey was featured in the *Western Citizen* as early as 1821.[57]

Rum

Rum, a so-called maritime liquor, also known in a previous life as *kill-devil* and subsequently *Rumbullion*, made from distilled molasses, deserves a mention for the significant part it plays in the story of the ascendency of whiskey, and spirits in general. In America, it was the drink of the colonial era and the Revolution. Molasses could be cultivated easily in coastal regions and had been for hundreds, if not thousands, of years. However, it was expensive to move inland and anyway, America's great interior was not such a ready molasses-producing zone. As settlers, migrants from Europe, in particular Scotland and Ireland, moved inland from the East Coast, and observed the vast wealth of corn and other cereal grains they realised that they could produce a different liquor far more easily and less expensively.

> *Always carry a flagon of whiskey in case of a snakebite and furthermore, always carry a small snake.* (W.C. Fields, 1880–1946)

Bourbon-laced legends[58]

Once, when Mark Twain was entering England, he told the Customs' Officer he had nothing to declare, and that his [suit] cases only held clothes. Searching, the officer found a bottle of Bourbon. 'Only clothes, Sir?' he queried ironically. 'Yes', replied Mark Twain, 'you are holding my nightcap'! [59]

The distinctive flavour of the charred barrels used in aging bourbon has some delightful propositions.

• One was that members of the distilling fraternity of the time acquired barrels from fishmongers who had scrubbed them out in order to on-sell them and into these the distillers put their liquor. Apparently a Baptist preacher, Elijah Craig, is associated with this tale. Some claim it is he who, looking for storage for his whiskey, invested in some herring barrels as they were all he could afford. He went on to torch their interiors in order to eliminate their sharp fishy odour. This done, it was not long before he cottoned on to the fact that the process of leaving whiskey in charred barrels for a period of time altered its flavour and colour in a most agreeable fashion.

• Another proposition was that a cooper accidently burned and charred his barrel-building timber and persisted in using it anyway. His barrels became the stock-in-trade for distillers who grew to like the flavour the charring produced in their liquor.

• There is also the tale of a farmer who stored some barrels of whiskey under his barn in order to age them. When his barn was burned to the ground, he dug up his precious trove and found the whiskey still in its barrels, but that it had acquired a rich new smooth and smoky flavour. Lucky for us, and for posterity!

63

So, between scrubbing and torching and a lot of initiative, somewhere along the line, a new style of whiskey emerged from a charred cask. Its flavour caught on and bourbon was born. While there is no means of substantiating these tales, the fact remains that charred barrels are now used in the production of bourbon as a matter of law. Although each barrel may only be used once in bourbon production, this does not stop their being exported to other whisky-making nations for ongoing use.

Sipping whiskeys

This is the term given to the more refined versions of bourbon: more refined because of enhanced filtering which necessarily takes more time. The outcome is uber mellow, perfect for sipping. *Jack Daniel's Whiskey* made in Tennessee is classified by some as a sipping whiskey. Interesting is the fact that *Jack Daniel's* is actually produced in a 'dry' county. While you may purchase your *Jack Daniel's* on site, you most definitely may not sample it there.

There are still approximately 200 'dry' counties in the USA. One specific town that is not dry however is Savannah, Georgia. When in Savannah you will find that spirits and wines flow aplenty. Plus the citizens of Savannah even have the quirky custom of encouraging their residents and guests to walk about their picturesque town brandishing their drinks in paper cups, and these come in all sizes! Glass is not allowed.

LYNCHBURG LEMONADE

This is named after Lynchburg, Tennessee, the hometown of the *Jack Daniel's Distillery*.
Serves: 1

Ingredients:
30ml (1oz) *Jack Daniel's Whiskey*
15ml (½oz) triple sec
1 tbs sugar syrup
1 tbs lemon, or lime, juice
Quantity lemon or lime soda

Method:
Pour whiskey, triple sec, sugar and juice into a Collins glass filled with ice.
Top up with soda and stir well.

Tennessee whiskey versus Kentucky bourbon

There are only four brands of Tennessee Whiskey that are currently bottled:

• *Jack Daniel's*
• *George Dickel*
• *Benjamin Prichard's*
• *Collier and McKeel*

It appears that there is an interminable debate about the contrasts and sameness of Tennessee whiskey and Kentucky bourbon (or bourbon whiskey). All bourbon, by the way, is not made in Kentucky alone. It is distilled in several states as mentioned earlier (Tennessee, Virginia, Missouri. California, Georgia, Illinois, Indiana, Ohio and Pennsylvania.) Only Kentucky, however, legally has the right to have the state's name on the label as a 'bourbon' product, in the manner of champagne.

Charles [Chuck] Cowdery, whiskey connoisseur, expert in all things related to 'whiskey' in America, and blogger extraordinaire, has in his own words spent a lot of time looking into this debate and studied all the laws, bi-laws and regulations controlling the nomenclature of these two varieties. In his blog dated January 2012 he states:

> *Tennessee whiskey isn't any whiskey made in Tennessee. The [Tennessee] whiskey must meet all of the requirements for Straight Bourbon Whiskey [as laid down by federal regulators] and be made [specifically] in Tennessee to qualify. [Again, like champagne.]*

Cowdery has also said that to pitch 'bourbon whiskey' against 'Tennessee whiskey' is a 'distinction without a difference'.

> *It is similar to the whiskey/whisky spelling delineation, because it is one of those essentially trivial issues that ignorant people pontificate about … pick one and stick with it.*

I concur. Cowdery says *Jack Daniel's* and *George Dickel* are bourbon in all but name. They are the same type and their difference is merely technical. Tennessee whiskey remains 'inside the profile' of straight bourbon whiskey. *Van Winkle Special Reserve 12 Year Old* is an example of a Kentucky straight bourbon whiskey.

My forebears come from Alabama. In fact, I have a large number of relatives still living there. However, even though Alabama's state spirit is whiskey, the term 'Alabama whiskey' may not be used since it is produced in Kentucky, not Alabama.

America spells whiskey, as we are all aware, with an 'e'. However Kentucky spells it without an 'e' because Kentucky whisky is made after the Scottish style using cold winter wheat, and not summer wheat. In this manner, Kentucky honours the Scottish ways and uses Scottish spelling too. Maker's Mark and Early Times spell their whisky just like that: whisky.

However Kentucky bourbon whiskey is another matter. *Maker's Mark*, made from a mash that consists of 51% corn, red winter wheat and malted barley is distilled twice (as are most bourbons) again, in the style of their Scottish distilling cousins.

Kentucky county and the much-fêted Mint Julep

Think Mint Julep, and the Kentucky Derby springs to mind. Or vice-versa. This famous race is contested annually, on the first Saturday in May, in Louisville, Kentucky, and has been so since 1875. It is a race for three-year-old thoroughbreds. The course is two kilometres, or one and a quarter miles. In America, the race is known variously as 'the most exciting two minutes in sport' or 'the Run for Roses' as the winner is draped in a blanket of roses.

The Julep dates back to the fifteenth century when herbs, sugar and water were blended into a medicinal cocktail. This modest infusion in turn developed into something a little more potent with the use of brandy and mint, or sometimes, peach brandy, or even Cognac. Then in 1875, the year of the first Derby in Kentucky, the bourbon of that name became the base alcohol of choice.

Only premium bourbons are recommended for this drink: *Maker's Mark** (part of the Beam stable), *Knob Creek* (same), or *Woodford Reserve* (which incidentally is distilled in copper stills imported from Scotland.)[60]

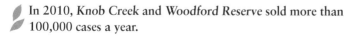 In 2010, Knob Creek and Woodford Reserve sold more than 100,000 cases a year.

*Maker's Mark is in the press as I write.[61] They recently diluted the alcoholic content of their Kentucky straight bourbon whisky from 45% to 42% ABV (90 to 84 proof) because, to quote their chairman, Bill Samuels Jnr,

'Demand for our bourbon was exceeding our ability to make it'. The dilution underwhelmed their customers and the distillers promptly restored the strength of their bourbon to its traditional level.

The focus of the Julep is not just the alcohol base however. There is endless discussion about what to do with and how to prepare the mint.

Some say that the key is in the placement of the mint which should be extended above the rim to allow one to inhale the aroma while sipping the bourbon. Some, however, prefer to muddle the mint first to infuse the bourbon with its aromatic fragrance. Extreme mint aficionados will go so far as to infuse a bottle of bourbon with a few cups of mint leaves … [62]

TRADITIONAL SOUTHERN-STYLE MINT JULEP

Serves: 1

Ingredients:
120ml (4oz) Kentucky bourbon
1 tsp sugar syrup
4–6 sprigs mint

Method:
Pour the liquid ingredients into a Julep cup [the traditional Julep cup was made in silver] or a Collins glass filled with crushed ice. Stir well until the glass becomes frosty. Garnish with mint sprigs, placing them over the rim.</recipe>

MUDDLED MINT JULEP

Serves: 1

Ingredients:
12–14 fresh mint leaves
1 tsp sugar syrup

120ml (4oz) Kentucky bourbon
Twist of lemon peel (optional)

Method:
Muddle the mint leaves and syrup in the bottom of a chilled Julep cup or old-fashioned glass. Fill the glass with crushed ice, add the bourbon and stir until the glass is frosty. Garnish with sprigs of mint extending them above the rim. A twist of lemon peel may be added.

FROZEN MINT JULEP
Serves: 1

Ingredients:
6 small mint leaves
180ml (3oz) Kentucky bourbon
40ml (1oz) fresh lemon juice
40ml sugar syrup
1 mint sprig

Method:
Muddle the mint leaves with the bourbon, lemon juice and sugar syrup in the bottom of a small glass. Pour the mixture into a blender, add the ½ cup crushed ice and blend until slushy. Pour into a chilled old-fashioned glass and garnish with the mint sprig.

Whiskey and bourbon consumption is booming in Russia. *Jack Daniels* has 72% market share of all the alcohol purchased and drunk in Russia, followed by *Jim Beam*. I am a great fan of vodka, but I am glad the Russians are broadening their horizons.

Chapter 8

America's back-story: pot stills, rebellions and Prohibition

I like whiskey. I always did, and that is why I never drink it. (Robert E. Lee, 1807–1870)

1791: Interestingly there are more than 5,000 pot stills in full working order in western Pennsylvania at this time. That amounts to one for every six people.

1794: The Whiskey Rebellion or Whiskey Insurrection breaks out. Its first stirrings date to 1791. Historically whisky had been used as rural currency. It was traded for essentials such as salt, sugar, iron, powder and shot. It was given as pay to farm workers, used in birth and death rituals and also consumed whenever legal documents were signed. It was also given to jurors in court and to voters by political campaigners. Clergymen received their stipend in similar liquid form.

> *We got more provision for our whiskey than the same money, which we paid for the liquor, would have bought; so after all it proved a very profitable investment. (Buffalo Bill, 1846–1917)*

Thus, when an excise tax was levied against the production of distilled drinks in 1791 by US Treasury Secretary Alexander Hamilton, to help pay off the massive national debt brought about by the Revolution (1775–1783), the people (many of them farmer-distillers) felt they had little choice but to revolt. About 500 men, 'whiskey boys' gathered at Braddock's Head and this motley group expanded into an impromptu army of 6,000 (whose modest aspiration was to secede from the US and form an independent state).

President George Washington orders 13,000 militiamen to subdue the uprising and to the huge relief of everyone, [understatement], it is quelled successfully. Indeed, when the insurgents hear the militiamen approaching, they hurry home and withdraw from any actual confrontation. Apparently a token group of about 20 men is arrested but not held for long. All are duly pardoned. Ironically, the taste for whiskey develops considerably at this time because it is doled out to the soldiers as a perk for following orders. Understandably, they develop an enthusiasm for it.

1800: Thomas Jefferson's Republican party comes to power and repeals the whiskey tax. Collective relief.

...

1920: Prohibition is declared in the US. All sales of alcohol are banned nationwide, the only exemption being for whiskey prescribed through licensed pharmacies.

Doctors stand to augment their incomes by very little work filling out prescriptions for 'whiskey-remedies' during this period of enforced sobriety. Small wonder then that the popular 'Walgreen' pharmacy chain grows during this time from a modest 20 retail stores to almost 400! [63]

1933: Prohibition is repealed via the Twenty-First Amendment, and the opportunity now presents itself for fortunes to be made by those who had artfully sharpened their distilling skills during those dark thirteen years.

Cocktail wizardry was a fiery force during Prohibition. Skilled bartenders in underground speakeasies would compete to mask the distasteful flavour of low-grade moonshine by inventing increasingly exotic blends to please the palate: some with singular names: The Scofflaw, for instance. Scofflaw took its name from the Scofflaws, those who made it their business to flout the law.

THE SCOFFLAW

According to Nigel, a friend and part-time mixologist, this cocktail was debuted at Harry's Bar in Paris in 1924 and swiftly found its way across the Atlantic to those targeted by what is sometimes referred to as America's 'noble experiment'.

Serves: 1

Ingredients:
45ml (1½oz) rye whiskey
20ml (¾oz) lemon juice
30ml (1oz) dry vermouth
20ml (¾oz) grenadine
1 dash of Angostura bitters

Method:
Combine all ingredients in a shaker.
Shake well and pour over ice in whatever scoffing glass you most enjoy.
Add a twist of lemon if you are feeling adventurous.

It was not only the bartenders of the time who were exercising their creative muscles. Despite regulation, the consumption of alcohol was epidemic. Thousands died from 'bathtub' liquor. Cargo had to be camouflaged, taxmen had to be outwitted and outrun: everyone was being tested. All of which naturally built up something of a thirst.

Classic whisky cocktails
RUSTY NAIL
Serves: 1

Ingredients:
60ml (2oz) Blended Scotch whisky
60ml (2oz) Drambuie
Lemon rind (optional)

Method:
Fill your favourite tumbler with crushed ice.
Pour over the other ingredients and stir.

WHISKY MAC
Utterly delicious and familiar too as a hearty and reliable cold remedy like those Irish toddies. Ginger has long been recognised as the carrier of many healthy properties.

Serves: 1

Ingredients:
60ml (2oz) Blended Scotch whisky
60ml (2oz) Ginger wine

Method:
Fill your favourite tumbler with crushed ice.
Pour over the other ingredients and stir.

HIGHBALL
The highball apparently took its name from a railway signal in which a raised ball on a pole signalled the driver to accelerate because his train was running late. The interpretation of 'hurry up' then morphed into the name of a drink

that could be reliably and swiftly produced. Typically it is made as follows combining a spirit (in this instance whiskey) and a sparkling mixer (soda or ginger ale) in a tall glass.

The tall glass keeps the fizz alive for longer. I had never considered that before.

Serves: 1

Ingredients:
60ml (2oz) whiskey (or Scotch whisky)
150ml (5oz) club soda or ginger ale

Method:
Pour ingredients into a tall glass over ice (or not) according to your taste.

OLD FASHIONED
This is the perfect way to start out or to conclude an evening. The maraschino cherry, I recently have learned, is absolutely *de rigueur* although it is not generally to my taste. However, what makes an Old Fashioned such a triumph is the fact that it is not too sweet; has a lot of bite and is a splendid mood-enhancer.

Serves: 1

Ingredients:
60ml (2oz) bourbon, Scotch or rye whiskey
1 slice orange
1 sugar cube
2 dashes Angostura Bitters
1 splash water
1 maraschino cherry

Method:
Muddle whisky with slice of orange.
Pop the sugar cube in a cocktail glass.
Splash on the Angostura Bitters.
Add your muddled whiskey and water.

MANHATTAN

It is rumoured that a bartender invented what has become a classic
New York cocktail at a party at the Manhattan Hotel hosted by
Clementine, Sir Winston Churchill's mother.

> *The water was not fit to drink. To make it palatable, we had to add
> whisky. By diligent effort, I learnt to like it.* (Sir Winston Churchill,
> 1874–1965)

Serves: 1

Ingredients:
60ml (2oz) Canadian rye whiskey or bourbon whisky
30ml (1oz) sweet vermouth
2 dashes Angostura Bitters
1 maraschino cherry and orange zest

Method:
Pour the liquid ingredients into a shaker with ice.
Shake and strain into a martini glass.
Garnish with the maraschino cherry and orange zest.
NB. Manhattans are also drunk over ice.

Bogey's remedy and his big mistake

In 1950, when *The African Queen* was being filmed in the Congo, everybody in the crew, including Katherine Hepburn, went down with dysentery because of the undrinkable water. The only individual to escape the shocking illness was Humphrey Bogart who drank, naturally enough, only whiskey.

Bogart's last words when he died in 1957 were:

I never should have switched from Scotch to Martinis.

Big mistake.

Chapter 9

A light distillation and retrospective of Europe's whisky history

1478: The first printed book on the science of distillation by an Austrian doctor, Michael Puff von Schrick is published in Augsburg.

Von Schrick claimed that not only could a sip of *aqua vitae* taken every morning ward off illness, but taken on one's deathbed, afforded one a bonus gasp for one last utterance.

1500: Another noted book on distillation is published: *Liber de arte distillandi simplicia et composite*, also known as *The Little Book of Distillation* by Hieronymus Brunschwig, (also spelled Brunschwyck) a German physician, surgeon, chemist and pharmacologist.[64] From the sound of it Dr. Brunschwig was something of a Renaissance man. He was certainly a very busy man.

As well as describing the various methods and the apparatus for the distillation of plant and animal extracts, he provides a comprehensive list of maladies (including marital discord, poor memory, depression and issues surrounding inebriation) along with a corresponding list of distillates and extracts recommended for their management! I imagine he would be brilliant on talkback radio.

1505: The Guild of Surgeon Barbers is granted a monopoly on whisky production begging the question about the practice of barbers undertaking minor medical procedures ... (haunting visions of *Sweeny Todd* come to mind). Whisky, it appears, was used as both an anaesthetic and as an early type of antibiotic.

These surgeons could be construed as early pioneers of hairdressing. The red and white lights outside traditional barbers' shops (today's salons) continue to attest to the bandages and blood from those surgeons' practices, and those of the cutting edge whisky-drinking hairdressers of the day.

1530s: Henry VIII's dissolution of the church propels monks out from behind monasteries' walls and they take their craft with them.

The charms of *aqua vitae* and its agreeable de-stressing effects begin to bewitch the wider public. The monks however are not the only distillers.

Farmers begin to distil their own 'lively water' at home. This was drunk upon preparation, so was very coarse (*very lively*) by contrast to its later smoother and more refined descendent(s).

1608: A license to distil is granted to *The Old Bushmills Distillery* on the north coast of Ireland.

1638: The Worshipful Company of Distillers is set up to regulate and supervise the production of spirits in England.

1707: The Acts of Union merge Scotland and England.

1725: The extortionate English Malt Tax is introduced, and the cost of whisky skyrockets. Most of Scotland's distillation is shut down or forced underground. Not deterred however the distillers realise their booty simply requires camouflage, and nowhere is deemed too sacred: coffins, altars, anywhere and anything to escape the scrutiny of the inexhaustible taxman. Fake funeral processions are even arranged as a means of moving grog. Ministers, in on the game, warn the ever-prying taxman that the deceased died of small pox. This is a sure fire way of subduing their curiosity.

1750s: Moonshine is endemic. This bootlegging was so-named because the illicit spirit was distilled and sold under cover of night: 'by the light of the moon'. This was so smoke rising from stills was obscured from the inexorable eagle-eyed, taxman.

The three lads in the verse below, 'A Peck o' Maut' by Robert Burns (1759–1796), demonstrate the good cheer and imperturbability of the folk who liked a 'peck' at this time.

'Peck O' Maut' by Robert (Robbie) Burns

O, Willie brew'd a peck o' maut,
And Rob and Alan cam to see.
Three blyther hearts, that lee-long night,
Ye wad no found in Christendie.
Chorus
We are na fou, we'fe nae that fou,
But just a drappie in our e'e;
The cock may crow, the day may daw,
And ay we'll taste the barley bree.
Here are we met, three merry boys,
Three merry boys I trow are we;
And monie a night we've merry been,
And many mare we hope to be!
It is the moon, I ken her horn,
That's blinkin in the lift sae hie;
She shines sae bright to wyle us hame,
But, by my sooth, she'll wait a wee!
Wha first shall rise to gang awa,
A cuckold, coward loun is he!
Wha first beside his chair shall fa',
He is the King amang us three!

The verse remained as popular as its subject, and is quoted decades later in
The Pickwick Papers by Charles Dickens. (1837)

I don't quite recollect how many tumblers of whisky toddy each man drank after supper; but this I know, that about one o'clock in the morning, the bailie's grown-up son became insensible while attempting the first verse of Willie brewed a peck o' maut.

1823: In England the Excise Act legalises the distillation of whisky (not without a tax of course), which in turn subdues the moonshine industry.

1831: Irishman, Aeneas Coffey, patents the Coffey Still that both simplifies the production of whisky and makes production less costly. The Irish distillers of the day choose not use Coffey's still because they believe the whisky produced to be inferior to that produced with pot stills. However, the Scots, possibly a tad more entrepreneurial, make extensive use of the new-styled still, and go on to develop methods for blending that self same 'inferior whisky' with that of better quality, and thus creating the first significant 'blends'. This introduction leads to the Scottish assuming market leadership.

I have been reliably informed by Bill Lark[65] that this is the juncture at which the Irish put the 'e' in their whiskey, because they wanted to differentiate their refined product from the blended Scottish rival. They lifted the 'e' from Coffey, and popped it into whiskey.

Chapter 10

Landmarks

I have heard it mentioned that in my grandmother's day *J&B Rare* was a wise choice for a lady because, while she may have given the appearance of sipping on something delicate, as befitting her pedigree, she was actually enjoying the fruits of a fairly stiff drink.

J&B Rare

J&B Rare is the first whisky I ever drank, so it marks a highpoint for me. And while it was a starting point for me, its own trajectory from its early days is an amazing one: the term trailblazer hardly covers it. *J&B Rare* is universally synonymous with top shelf quality. It is enjoyed for its silky smooth flavour and also its radiant, light golden colour. Here is an outline of its story.

1749: Justerini & Brooks Ltd. is founded by Giacomo Justerini and George Johnson in Pall Mall, London and *J&B Rare* is created and designated as their house whisky.

1760: Justerini and Johnson win the first of their nine Royal Warrants as suppliers of fine wines and spirits for the Royal Household for the celebrations surrounding the coronation of George III.

 Since 1760, Justerini and Brooks have been suppliers to every successive British Monarch.

1779: On June 17th *Usquebaugh* is advertised in *The Morning Post*, the first recorded advertisement in the history of Justerini and Brooks.

1930s: Eddie Tatham, Managing Director UK, and originator of *J&B Rare*, because of his audacity, has a spell behind bars in America. His enthusiasm to market Justerini and Brooks' whisky to those under the thumb of Prohibition earns him a severe dressing down. Even the provision of tasting samples is strictly against regulations.

1933: In triumph, once Prohibition is repealed, *J&B Rare* is formally exported to America and Justerini and Brooks Ltd. is clearly identified as the leading Scotch whisky brand in the eastern United States of America.

1950s: Frank Sinatra, Dean Martin and Sammy Davis Jr. all put *J&B Rare* in the limelight during their shows in Los Angeles.

1960s: Justerini and Brooks appoint distributors and agents around the world.

1962: *J&B Rare* is exported to Spain where it very soon becomes the country's No. 1 whisky.

1963: One million cases of *J&B Rare* are sold to America.

1970s: *J&B Rare* is now fully established in Europe

1972–1993: Justerini and Brooks go on to earn the accolade of the Queen's Award for Export Achievement no less than six times.

2000: With over 160 distributors, *J&B Rare* is recognised as the second most popular Scotch whisky in the world, and the No. 1 in Europe.

Today its major markets are Spain, America, South Africa, Italy, South America and Asia.[66]

The Distillers Company

It is amazing to see the power of the species; how the industry of Scottish whisky was originally an alliance of families, which became an association, which grew into a company, and finally graduated into a conglomerate. Diageo is now the world's biggest whisky producer with twenty-eight malt distilleries, and two grain distilleries. It also owns the world famous Gleneagles Hotel and a 34% share in the Moët Hennessy drinks division of Louis Vuitton Moët Hennessy.

1759: Arthur Guinness signs the lease on the St. James' Gate brewery in Dublin.

1865: A trade association calling itself The Scotch Distillers' Association is formed.

1877: The Scotch Distillers' Association becomes The Distillers Company plc. The Scottish Distilleries (MacFarlane & Co., John Bald & Co., John Haig & Co., MacNab Bros & Co., Robert Mowbray and Stewart & Co.) are all involved having previously, all of them, headed up the whisky business in Scotland.

1925: The Distillers Company plc merges with John Walker & Son and Buchanan-Dewar.

1960s: The company flat-lines after diversifying into pharmaceuticals and promoting the drug thalidomide. This drug was prescribed to pregnant women with the intention of helping them overcome morning sickness but led in fact most tragically to their babies being deformed.

1986: An employee of Guinness leads a takeover of The Distillers Company plc. and promises that the about-to-be United Distillers, under the banner of Guinness, will have its headquarters in Edinburgh. The promise is not kept, the employee of Guinness is dispatched to jail for insider trading, and the company is later rebranded as Diageo (its headquarters remaining in Park Royal, West London).

Diageo plc
1997: Diageo plc conglomerate is created through the merger of Grand Metropolitan and Guinness. It comprises the world's greatest collection of premium drinks.

Diageo plc sells its products in over 180 countries and has offices in around eighty countries. It owns many whisky brands such as:

- *Johnnie Walker*, the No. 1 Scotch whisky in the world according to the IWSR .
- *J&B Rare*, the No. 5 Scotch whisky in the world, according to the IWSR. France is its greatest market (whisky's second biggest market in the world).
- *Buchanan's* and *Old Parr* (sold chiefly in Latin America[67])
- *Bushmills* (Ireland)
- *Crown Royal* (Canada)
- *Windsor* (sold in the Asia-Pacific Region[68])

   'The No. 1 'Super premium whisky'

(Diageo also own *Smirnoff*, *Baileys*, *José Cuervo*, *Tanqueray* and *Guinness*.)

Distilling in England and Wales

England has had something of a stop and start relationship with whisky. In the nineteenth century it had a number of distilleries that sent their whisky to Scotland for blending. These had closed down by the early twentieth century only to be given an opportunity of rising again under St. George's banner. The *St. George Distillery* was established in 2004, in Norfolk. According to Robin Lynam,[69] St. George's single malt whiskies have been highly praised, as have Cornwall's *Hicks and Healy's* single malt. In Wales, *Penderyn*, the only distillery now in existence there, produces *Penderyn Port Wood* single malt, which has also been recognised.[70]

Chapter 11

Australia

As I have been living in Australia for 30 years,
I am very proud to underline (fairly expansively)
Australia's significant contribution to the world
whisky story. Like the distilleries in Ireland and
Scotland, the distilleries mentioned in this chapter
are destinations in and of themselves. All have
a wealth of colour and history as well as some
pretty stunning malts. There are other Australian
distilleries, which while not highlighted in the
text, most certainly do warrant a reconnaissance.
Among these are *Great Southern* and *Limeburners*
in West Australia, *Smith's Angaston* in South
Australia, *The Australian* in New South Wales and
Belgrove in Tasmania; not for a moment wanting
to overlook a further range of emerging artisan
distilleries all of which contribute to the narrative.
(*Black Gate* in New South Wales, *Castle Glen
Australia* in Queensland, *Corowa Whisky Distillery*
in New South Wales and *New World Whisky
Distillery* in Victoria.)

TASMANIA

'The Godfather of the Australian Whisky Industry' and Lark Distillery

Bill Lark is the founder of *Lark Distillery* (1992) and is referred to by many as 'The Godfather of the Australian Whisky Industry'.[71] He has forged a fascinating path in the business of whisky and has generously helped his whisky cohort along the way. Early on he saw that Tasmania had everything to offer that would conspire to make wonderful whisky, and for twenty years *Lark Distillery* has been doing just that. Bill had first to obtain a distillation license. This was only possible once he succeeded in having overturned Tasmania's one hundred and fifty-three-year ban on distilling. This was no easy task.[72] More recently he co-founded the Tasmanian Distillers Group along with seven other distilleries on the island.[73]

Much of Australia's whisky production is carried out on this small isle. Less now the 'Apple Isle' as it was formerly known, rather more the 'Whisky Isle'! Its air is beautifully clean, its water unpolluted, and world-class Franklin barley is cultivated there. *Lark Distillery* in Mount Pleasant, in addition to all this, has the distinction of having its own peat bog.[74]

 For the privilege of 'mining' their peat, the team at Lark has to pay a cheeky annual royalty of $13.50. (£9.25 or $14.00 USD.)

Tasmanian peat

Bill notes that the Tasmanian peat's character is subtly different from its Scottish counterpart, and that they [at Lark's] also make use of it in a specific way. 'No other distillery in Australia peat smokes their malt using Tasmanian peat in the manner we do'. Bill actually custom built his own smoker (advice on which has since been taken by some Scottish distillers). Rewardingly, their specific process of peat smoking malt is also drawing serious attention from Scotland where Bill's daughter Kristy has been invited to expand on the specifics of Lark's methods.

> *I know the whisky market has been dominated by the large international whisky companies, but I still believe the market for hand crafted whiskies[75] will have the strongest growth in the foreseeable future.*
> (Bill Lark)

Lark Distillery specifically matures its malt whiskies in small 'quarter' casks[76] that deliver a richer flavour than larger more traditional casks. (This follows because the ratio, or exposure, of liquid to wood is so much higher than that in larger casks.) The first barrel Bill and his wife Lyn filled was with liquor from a 75-litre still designed by Bill himself!

Whisky from *Lark Distillery* has deservedly found its way to Europe, America and Asia. The main offering in the Lark range is their *Single Cask Malt Whisky* at 43% but they have also *Distillers Selection* at 46% and *Cask Strength* at 58%. All of which I have tasted with the greatest of pleasure.

In addition to their own operation Lark on-sell some of their spirit and Heartwood have bottled and marketed *Velvet Hammer* at 68% ABV and *Convict Unchained* at no less than 71.9% ABV. I cannot resist the names but have yet to try the spirits.

Redlands
Bill and Lyn Lark are currently sharing their expertise with Amelia Hope and her husband James Reid in a brilliant whisky initiative, centred at Redlands.

Redlands, half an hour out of Hobart, is operating a distillery, but not just any distillery. This enterprise will cover every aspect of whisky production from go to whoa. Barley will be grown, harvested, malted, fermented, distilled and aged on site. Its distillery is housed in the heritage-listed, convict-built Georgian oast house and granary that make up part of the estate.

Redlands is an exquisite historic rural estate on the banks of the Plenty River in the Derwent Valley, established in 1819. This land was granted to George Frederick Read, son of George IV.

Young George was not recognised by the Crown because his mother, Prince George's first wife, was Catholic. Young George was thus dispatched to make his fortune carrying the rather more modest name of his wet nurse 'Read'.

Between the 1860s and 1970s Redlands was a thriving hop and grain farm leading to its premier position in the history of hop farming in Tasmania. It had its own cobblestone village including a bakery, store, butcher and bell tower to serve the 200 workers and their families who resided there during the hop-picking season.

The property also used to operate a dairy, apple orchard, wool yards, and a piggery no less. Not only does Redlands boast breathtaking early convict architecture but also some of the oldest European trees in Australia, including one of the biggest magnolia trees. To me the most eye-catching feature is the chain of waterways that runs like a maze across the property delivering crystal clear water to the property from the Plenty River. Convicts hand-dug over five kilometres of canals through Redlands, the first farm in Tasmania to be fully irrigated using gravity. Incredibly, some of these canals were actually lined with huon pine.

Tasmania Distillery and *Sullivan's Cove Single Malt*

Tasmania Distillery produces *Sullivan's Cove Single Malt*. *Tasmania Distillery* was established in 1994 at the cove of its name, on the site where the British first settled Hobart on the Derwent River. Today it is one of Australia's most recognised whisky brands. *Sullivan's Cove* is also Australia's most awarded whisky having secured many 'Golden Liquid' awards through Jim Murray.

Jim Murray also named *Sullivan's Cove* 'Southern Hemisphere Whisky of the Year' in his 2013 *Whisky Bible*, after French Oak Cask HH509 was awarded 96.5, the highest score for an Australian whisky. *Sullivan's Cove* was also named 'World Whisky Grand Master' at the 2012 Spirits Masters in London.

Sullivan's Cove Single Malt has come of age under its chief distiller Patrick Maguire, who is a fourth generation son of Tasmanians. Locally grown barley and unpolluted soft water from the Mount Wellington area are used by the Cascade Brewery to make *Sullivan's Cove's* wash. Maguire has also perfected two-cask types (French oak port and American oak bourbon, the latter sourced from *Jim Beam*, *Jack Daniel's* and *Heaven Hill* distilleries) creating a deeper and more complex whisky than is achievable in just one wood. *Sullivan's Cove* single malt being bottled today is selected from the most superior of their barrels. Each bottle is filled, capped and labelled by hand. It is a delight to drink.

Old Hobart Distillery, one of the southernmost distilleries in the world

This is a family-run boutique business set up in 2007 and headed by Casey Overeem. The distillery, located in Blackmans Bay, Tasmania, is one of the most southern in the world.* Casey Overeem having paid visits to both Scotland and interestingly Norway, drew inspiration from both regarding techniques for distillation and he brought this home to Tasmania. Their single cask, single malt whisky is matured in casks that have previously contained port, bourbon or sherry.[77] Among their expressions are *Port Matured Single Cask*, *Single Malt Whisky* at 40% and also 60% (cask strength) ABV that has been aged in quarter cask barrels and *Sherry Matured Single Cask*, *Single Malt Whisky* also at 43% and 60% (cask strength) ABV that has also been aged in quarter casks.

Since the first release of *Overeem Single Malt Whisky* in December 2011, the whisky has received a number of national and international awards. These include:

• Liquid Gold Award (95 points) — Jim Murray's *Whisky Bible* 2013
• Australia's Best Whisky 2012 — Malt Whisky Society of Australia
• Australasian Whisky of the Year 2012 — World of Whisky
• Silver Medal Winner (x3) — Wizards of Whisky, London 2012

* William McHenry & Sons Distillery (aka McHenry's) producers of (among other spirits) *Three Capes Single Malt Tasmanian Whisky* is the southernmost distillery.

Nant Distillery in the Tasmanian Highlands

Located in Tasmania's central highlands in picturesque Bothwell, *Nant* started its life as an old water-driven flourmill built by convicts in 1823. *Nant* CEO and Founder Keith Batt purchased the property in 2004 and began to convert the historic farmstead into a whisky distillery. This included refurbishing an old water-driven flourmill, also dating back to the 1820s, used now for grinding barley into grist.

The boutique distillery makes the most of its pristine location, handcrafting its premium single malt whisky on the Nant Estate using traditional pot still distillation methods, 100% Tasmanian brewer's barley, and water sourced from from a one-million-year-old glacial lake via the Clyde River.

It is from these local ingredients that *Nant Single Malt Whisky* (American oak bourbon wood) achieved a 95.5 rating in Jim Murray's 2012 *Whisky Bible*, placing it among the top-ten tasting whiskies in the world.

> *Offering three single malt whisky expressions, French Oak Port, French Oak Sherry and American Oak Bourbon, maturation takes place in traditional American and French oak casks, which have previously held port, sherry or bourbon. It is from these casks that Nant whisky takes on its individual characteristics. Each individual cask is matured, decanted and hand bottled on the estate as a single cask maturation. The result is a unique Tasmanian Highland single malt whisky that captures the essence of Tasmania from which it has been created.* (Keith Batt)

Hellyer's Road, **Australia's largest distillery**

Established in 1996, *Hellyer's Road Distillery* is located in pristine farmlands on the North West Coast of Tasmania. It is a place that is normally associated with some of the finest dairy and vegetable produce found anywhere in the world. It is not usually synonymous with the production of premium single malt whisky. Despite this, *Hellyer's Road* is building a reputation domestically, and internationally, for producing a superb range of single malts. In 2010, its *Peated Single Malt* was judged the nation's best locally distilled single malt, and for the past two years it has met with excellent reviews at the prestigious *Whisky Live Fair* in Paris. In 2012, it released its first aged statement whisky, 1*0 Year Original*, and is currently exporting a range of whiskies to France.

The Roaring Forties

'The Roaring Forties' are the long-renowned prevailing westerly winds that carry to the distillery abundant but precious rain that is some of the world's purest water. This rainwater along with premium Tasmanian grain, and a maturing process that uses charred American oak casks, underpins the quality of this delightful range of single malts comprising *Original 10 Year, Original*, *Peated*, *Slightly Peated* and *Pinot Noir Finish* varieties.

HELLYER'S ROAD LEMON, LIME & WHISKY COCKTAIL

Serves: 1

Ingredients:
1 tsp Angostura Bitters
2 cups crushed ice
125ml (4fl oz) *Hellyer's Road Original Whisky*
1L (16fl oz) chilled lemonade
60ml (2oz) lime juice
60ml (2oz) lemon juice

Method:
Place ice in a large jug.
Pour all other ingredients over ice and stir thoroughly.

VICTORIA

Bakery Hill Distillery

Bakery Hill Distillery was established in 1999 when David Baker felt challenged to prove once and for all that great malt whisky could be made in Australia and not just in Scotland, as the Scots, he felt, liked to believe. Frustrated by reading endless pronouncements, that Scotland was the only nation capable of making exceptional quality single malt whisky because of their 'air and the water', David, an ex-biochemist, decided to prove them all wrong.

Why, he asked, could Australia not make its own world-class malts? It had succeeded with its wines and beers, and these were now eagerly sought after around the world, so why not its whiskies?

The challenge to produce a top quality malt whisky was compounded by the fact that a lot of general material written about its production was [in David's eyes] 'just plain incorrect'. So he spent two years experimenting and preparing small batches, to perfect his process and to make the adjustments necessary when accounting for Victoria's indigenous conditions.

Once his general process was fine-tuned, with careful yeast selection and fermenting conditions perfected, David purchased the most important component for the distillery, the still. Not wanting to leave this crucially important step to chance, the still was purchased following lengthy discussion with a renowned UK still engineering company.

Bakery Hill now produces unpeated malts (*Classic and Double Wood*) for six months of the year, and its peated range for the other six months. Unpeated malted barley is sourced and malted locally. The peated variety is imported.

> *Bakery Hill brews its wash to 8% ABV, double distils with the second 'cut' which is deliberately narrow to be sure to obtain the purity of flavour for which the distillery is now renowned. Maturation is completed in American oak ex-Tennessee whisky barrels with the double wood being finished for ten to twelve months in new French oak casks.*
> (David Baker)

The climatic conditions, specifically the higher [than typical Scottish] daily ambient temperatures near Mount Dandenong, ensure that one year in their bond stores is equivalent to nearly two years in an archetypal Scottish warehouse. And this is at the heart of the Australian whisky story. While Australia has so many features akin to Scotland, there are distinctions enough to provide the Antipodean whisky industry with some of its own singular attributes. Working effectively with these singularities is the core strength of the diverse and enterprising distillers in this region.

Describing the balance of *Bakery Hill Classic* Malt cask strength in his 2011 *Whisky Bible*, Jim Murray, gave it a score of 92 and said:

> *There are about twenty distilleries in Speyside that would die to be able to make whisky this stunningly integrated. Young, barely pubescent but sheer unadulterated class.*

High praise. David Baker would have surely been gratified that his aspirations to make whisky every bit as stylish as the distillers [do] in Scotland had been entirely fulfilled and with every good reason. And if he had any doubts, the following comment of Jim Murray's regarding the *Bakery Hill Double Wood 46%* that same year, would have surely put them to rest:

> *Balance, high class whisky is class whisky wherever it is made.*

Timboon Railway Shed Distillery **and** *Mountain Dew*

Steeped in history, this 'shed' of yore was brought back to life in 2007. It is located in Nirranda, near Warrnambool on the South West Coast of Victoria where in the late nineteenth century illicit distilling was at its peak, and a certain Tom Delaney was infamous for producing no less than 380 litres (100 gallons) of bootleg whisky a week; no mean feat. The locals praised the whisky as being 'smooth as new milk' and encouraged by this, Tom gave it the name of *Mountain Dew*. He was even impertinent enough to put a government stamp on all the bottles.

A detective inspector by the name of Christie was called in to stamp out the illicit industry, and disguising himself as a travelling tinker set about catching Tom and his companion in arms, Jim Love, and putting an end to their enterprise. In the manner of the Kelly legend, there was much skirmishing and carrying-on and while Tom was sadly defeated, bottles of *Mountain Dew* continued to turn up many years later.

Tim Marwood is the new proprietor at the *Timboon Shed Distillery*[78] and very significantly he reports:

> *Australian whiskies are developing a greater international appreciation due to the commitment and passion of people like Bill Lark. The Australian whisky market is developing and has the potential to grow and sustain this emerging micro industry. Our [Australia's] high evaporation rates contribute to a uniquely Australian style of malt.*

This is one of Australia's many singularities.

Australia's 'Champion Whisky', or *Corio*, an 'affordable spirit' [that needed heavy mixing]

My friend Jo mentioned *Corio Whisky* to me recently, and I have looked into its history. Corio was being distilled in a Geelong distillery owned by *Dewar's* in 1929.[79] The *Dewar* mandate was that on no terms was *Corio* ever to produce a whisky that bettered its Scottish cousins. This was no doubt frustrating for the distillers who would have naturally wanted to show off their craftsmanship and skill by producing a dram worth drinking, rather than the gut rot to which they were constrained.

Corio was widely mocked as being nothing more than Cor-10, the petrol of the day[80] as essentially it was as rough as hell. Furthermore, the aging process was construed as having been that of the travelling time between the distillery in Corio, Geelong, and the distributors in Melbourne, a distance of 68 kilometres or 42 miles! (In fact, it was aged for a minimum of five years.)

However, while quality could not be boasted, quantity could. The storage capacity at the distillery back in the 1940s was five million litres; that is one million, three thousand gallons![81] Today's Australian distilleries are unlikely to boast more than a two hundred thousand-litre storage capacity. *Corio* was at its peak between the 1940s and 1960s and apparently won many a trophy at agricultural shows, slightly begging the question: who were its competitors? Sadly, its production fell away during the 1970s and ultimately it was mothballed in 1980. It is rumoured that what remained of their stock was re-distilled into Vickers Gin. A sad denouement, but at least the spirit lived on to tell another tale.

Ned Kelly, distilling, digging and mangle-wurzel

Infamous Ned Kelly (immortalised by the great Australian artist Sidney Nolan) and the Kelly Gang were apparently not averse to distilling the odd dram o'maut themselves in among their other colourful exploits, the proceeds of which helped fund their multifarious shenanigans. Legend relates that they built and camouflaged a still near their hideout at Bullock Creek, near Mansfield, Victoria where they grew barley and mangle-wurzel[82] to ferment and distil their own exotic brew. They also had a gold mine for their sins.

NEW SOUTH WALES

Joadja, a canny Chinaman, and a whole lot of whisky going on

Joadja is an historic mining village located in the Southern Highlands, NSW, settled in the 1850s. In its day it was a thriving community boasting a post office, community hall, school, pharmacy, school of arts, cemetery, hotel and, allegedly, a French pastry chef and a Chinese grocer! Importantly it was home to four hundred Scottish families who, besides lending their skill to mining, also lent their skill to distilling some of Australia's earliest whisky. They were producing enough for their own needs, so had some to spare.

The artful Chinese grocer would routinely take his 'wares' to Sydney to sell at the markets there, and among his crates of oranges, he would conceal the moonshine — also for sale. The story goes that a code of practice was established between the Chinaman and the auctioneer auctioneering foodstuffs at the markets, which enabled sales to be made which were appropriate for the crated goods on offer. As a post-script it is thrilling to note that Joadja has recently been purchased and is being redeveloped. Whisky production in this beautiful region is promised once more; stills are being made in Hobart for the very purpose.

Chapter 12

Legends, superstitions and spells

There must be dozens, if not dozens of dozens, of legends surrounding disasters around calamities maritime involving precious cargoes of whisky and, of course, human life. Many whisky bottles carry personal tales of the mayhem that befell their forbears. If there is not one already, a book bearing all these tales is certainly warranted. Here however I include one in particular that has enduring mystery.

The S.S. Politician

In 1941 an 8,000-tonne cargo ship, the S.S. Politician, with a crew of 52, set off from Liverpool bound for Jamaica. She had at least 21,000 cases of Scotch whisky on board. Other reports suggest the number was actually as high as 250,000. (Thus why legends are legends.)

As she travelled north towards Scotland she ran aground on Calvay Island in the Sound of Eriskay, among the remote islands of the Outer Hebrides. The locals from neighbouring islands, Barra, Eriskay and South Uist apparently succeeded in rescuing over 9,000 cases of the whisky. Tantalisingly though not all of it was recovered from the sea floor, and is still there for the adventurous to discover. There have been numerous salvage missions, including one in the 1990s initiated by the Scottish company S.S. Politician PLC to excavate the sunken ship. I know not whether there remain any today to be excavated, but whisky keeps appearing.

Was the royal family on the point of flight in 1941?

This is not where the story ends however. There is a further legend behind the legend. A considerable amount of Jamaican currency (three million pounds[83] — in ten shilling notes) was also found on board the wreckage in 1941. More in fact than was estimated to be circulating in all of Jamaica itself at that time. To this day no one has been able to reason precisely why. The colony was in very poor shape. Possibly the money was being dispatched to reinforce the economy, or maybe it was going to be used to bribe a certain Alexander Bustamente, a native Jamaican, hostile to colonial rule? It was also speculated at the time that the British Royal family might have been planning to escape the Blitz. All of these are hypotheses and nothing was ever proved. What remains certain however is the mighty endurance of that cargo of whisky.

A Scot by the name of James Cameron owns a croft near the wreckage of the S.S. Politician today, and tells how his grandfather buried cases of the whisky when the ship first went down, but then forgot their location. The same holds true for plenty of other locals. Happily, cases have been emerging over time: apparently some turned up as recently as 2005.

Today you can buy *Calvay Mist*. It replicates the look and style of the cargo from the S.S. Politician.

This whole story has been immortalised in both film (**Whisky Galore**) and the book, **Whisky Galore** (1947), by Sir Compton McKenzie and a newer publication, by Arthur Swinson, *Scotch on The Rocks: The True Story behind Whisky Galore*, (Luath Press, 2005).

Whisky, a knighthood and a revival

Three bottles of *MacKinlay's* whisky are currently on their way back to the Antarctic after what has been strictly a round-trip visit to Scotland. These bottles, discovered in 2007 by a group of researchers, were in crates under floorboards in an expedition base used by Ernest Shackleton during his 1907 'Nimrod' excursion to the Antarctic. The crates, originally numbering 25, were frozen solid and yet the researchers could hear the whisky sloshing around inside the bottles after 100 years. The ambient temperature of minus 30°C (86°F) was simply not enough to freeze the spirit. The *MacKinlay* blend as it was quickly identified had been bottled in 1898 and aged for a full 15 years. Nirvana.

Sadly, the Nimrod explorers did not make it to the South Pole but set a record in 1909 when they made their way to the southernmost latitude ever reached, only 156 kilometres (97 miles) from their goal. Ernest Shackleton deservedly won a knighthood after this particular expedition. It's my belief the whisky deserves one too.

While it was unanimously agreed that the bottles would not be opened, a study was made of their contents in order to revive the blend. *Distiller Whyte & Mackay*, which now owns the *MacKinlay* brand, chartered a private jet to take the bottles from the Antarctic operations headquarters in Christchurch, New Zealand, to Scotland for analysis in 2011. Master Blender Richard Paterson who works with *Whyte & Mackay* was brought in to assist.

The original recipe had been lost but ingeniously Richard extracted a sample of the original whisky by inserting a syringe into one of the bottles between its neck and the cork. The alcohol was found to be 47.3% ABV. Richard's keen nose picked up 'soft, elegant, sherry wood flavours, and the peaty aromas of Speyside'. From this sample he was able to replicate the whisky exactly. *Whyte & Mackay* went on to recreate it in a limited edition of 50,000 bottles.[84] Each was priced at approximately $152AUD or $157USD but happily 5% of the proceeds of every bottle sold went to the conservation work of the Antarctic Heritage Trust.

More knighthoods deserved methinks.

The Jura Superstition
This is not merely a superstition but also the name given to a whisky made on the Isle of Jura. Jura (home to thousands of red deer — 'Jura') lies off the west coast of Scotland, has a population of 189 people and boasts one distillery. One of their celebrated whiskies is *Jura Superstition*. This brand of whisky carries an embossed ankh cross on every bottle, the ancient Egyptian

symbol promising good fortune. When pouring a dram the pourer is cautioned to always position the centre of their hand directly over the ankh cross, so as to ensure good fortune, or by contrast, to insure against bad.

> *Jura Superstition: The nose, chocolate covered peat. There's not really much smoke here, just an earthy, slightly medicinal peatiness coupled with notes of chocolate fudge, burnt toffee and vanilla. Behind that, stewed raisins, candied orange, and roasted nuts. Subtler notes of polished oak and faint smouldering grass hover in the background….*

Incidentally the *Isle of Jura Distillery* is due to release a 30-year-old whisky called *Camas an Staca*, taking its name from the largest standing stone on Jura of the same name. It has been aged for twenty-seven years in American oak and three in sherry casks. According to Jura's own website, the colour is 'dark walnut', its nose 'whispers of sea spray, spicy apple and honeyed figs', and its taste is of 'fleshy oranges, tangy liquorice and pineapple, followed by orange rind, black cherries, dark toffee and sundried raisins'. I hope one day I may try it.

🔥 If you want your customer to have an insatiable thirst for whisky, simply bury a bottle of whisky beneath his or her house and then reclaim the bottle, and toss it violently into a burning fire. Your customer's thirst is guaranteed.

Chapter 13

Whisky pairing with food, recipes and cocktails

In my view whisky can never diminish the pleasure of any food or more importantly, nor can it be compromised by sipping it while eating. To the contrary it seems to me that whisky goes well with everything even though this is possibly a dangerous precept for one's liver. There is however one exception I know of. Whisky does not work too well mixed with bran. A bold attempt was made by my friend Yvonne to make her dry and dusty cereal just the tiniest bit palatable. She remains unpersuaded.

Robert Hicks, master blender, advocates whisky with spicy Indian food, also smoked cheese, spiced meat and fish. Fiona Beckett[85] has made some suggestions and references Dave Broom, Glaswegian whisky author and expert. She proposes many a happy marriage between food and whisky, and also reminds us that a bit of water will help the whisky work best with these foods:

Light, fragrant whiskies that have a 'touch of sweetness' blend well with the following:

• Sushi, smoked salmon, dressed crab, Cullen skink (smoked haddock soup), cock-a-leekie (clear chicken and leek soup), parsnip soup, kedgeree and soft creamy cheeses.

Medium-bodied whiskies 'with some peat influence' complement:

• Smoked mackerel, smoked mussels, smoked oysters, smoked duck, smoked venison, duck or chicken liver pâté, seared scallops, haggis, roast or braised pheasant, or guinea fowl.

Full-bodied rich whiskies 'aged in sherry casks or European oak', align well with:

• Seared or grilled steak, roast pork and venison, rich fruity cakes, why not Christmas pudding? All assorted pies and puddings: mince pies, pecan pies, sticky date puddings, gingerbread, biscuits, such as chocolate or ginger snaps or brownies and cheeses, cheddars and washed-rind.

Dave Broom advocates 'Scallops and bacon and dark chocolate (not on the same plate obviously) with a peaty whisky.' Also he encourages: anchovy-based spreads and dips, hot-smoked salmon, haggis, tea-smoked chicken, mature cheddar and strong blue cheeses, especially Roquefort.

Did I say that whisky pairs well with anything? I have obviously not checked all the above combinations but am happy to try them out. Meanwhile please enjoy the following recipes with which you may drink whisky, while also making use of whisky in the cooking.

A WHISKY-INSPIRED GLAZE FOR YOUR HAM

I think you never lose by being excessively generous and assiduous with basting roast meats. So doubling up on the ingredients below might be a good plan.

Serves: A good basting for a more than average weight of ham

Ingredients:
¼ cup whisky
½ cup light brown sugar
½ cup apple cider
¼ cup Dijon mustard
1 tsp ground black pepper
¾ tsp allspice

Method:
Over low heat whisk together in a small saucepan the whisky, sugar and apple cider.

Once sugar is completely dissolved remove from heat and stir in mustard, pepper and allspice.

Voilà, your whisky-based basting sauce, and don't forget to insert cloves across the back of your ham.

AN ALTERNATIVE GLAZE

Serves: As above

Ingredients:
½ cup seeded mustard
½ cup light brown sugar
⅓ cup honey
1 tsp Tabasco sauce
1½ cups whisky — for the pan

Method:
Whisk ingredients together in a bowl.
Use 1½ cups whisky (or bourbon) in the base of your cooking pan while you are cooking the ham to infuse it with aromas that only whisky or bourbon can provide!

BRAISED ONIONS WITH BOURBON

This is such an easy way of jazzing up a roast or BBQ, a fabulous accompaniment to any meat dish in fact, especially beef or pork.
Serves: 4

Ingredients:
2 tbs butter
2 tbs olive oil
4 large onions cut into 2cm (1") slices
1 tsp salt
½ tsp freshly ground pepper
¼ cup beef stock
¼ cup bourbon or whisky

Method:
Melt butter and oil together in a heavy based pan.
Raise heat and sear onions for two minutes.
Add salt and pepper and stock and stir in well.
Reduce heat and simmer for 10–12 minutes.
Add bourbon and gently reduce for three minutes.

WHISKY AND PECAN LOAF

This is simple and delicious and takes barely any time at all to prepare. It has all my favourite flavours: whisky, coffee, almond and pecan.
Serves: 12–15

Ingredients:
¼ cup vegetable oil
2 large eggs
1½ tsp almond essence
1½ cups sour cream
½ cup whisky/bourbon
1 cup packed light brown sugar
2¼ cups plain flour
2¼ tsp baking powder
½ tsp baking soda
½ tsp salt
1½ tsp ground nutmeg
1 tsp instant coffee powder (espresso is best)
   and 1 tbs boiling water to dissolve it (or one shot of espresso)
1¼ cups chopped pecans and/or walnuts

Method:
Heat oven to 175° (340°).
Gently beat together the oil, eggs, almond essence.
Add sour cream, bourbon (or whisky) and sugar. Mix well.
Fold in sifted flour, baking powder, baking soda, salt and nutmeg.
Dissolve coffee in a couple of tablespoons of hot water and stir into mixture.
(Or one shot of espresso).
Finally fold in chopped nuts.
Spoon mixture into a lined loaf tin and bake at 175° (340°) for
approximately 45 minutes.
Cool in the tin before turning out onto wire rack to cool.

CHOCOLATE CHESTNUT AND BOURBON CAKE WITH BOURBON CHANTILLY CREAM

This looks like a whopper of a recipe but it really is quite straightforward.
You do need to set aside a bit of time though. It's a great party piece
welcomed by all ages.

(NB. Bourbon may readily be substituted with whisky)
Serves: 10

Ingredients:
6 eggs separated
2 extra egg yolks
1½ cups caster sugar (plus ⅓ cup extra)
4 tbs whisky/bourbon (plus 2 tsp extra)
2½ cups chestnut purée (crème de marrons)
¾ cup ground pecans (plus pecan pieces for decoration)
2 tsp instant coffee dissolved in 1 tbs boiling water
120g (4½oz) chilled butter cut into pieces

40g (1½oz) dark chocolate, chopped
400g (¾ pound) dark chocolate in bits
3½ cups whipping cream
½ cup icing sugar

Method:

Cake

Heat oven to 180° C (350°F).

Grease and line 2 x 22cm (9") cake tins.

Beat 6 egg yolks thoroughly and stir in 1½ cups sugar and 1½ tsp bourbon.

Fold in 2 cups chestnut purée.

Stir in ground pecans.

Whip egg whites with a pinch of salt until stiff.

Fold egg whites into batter.

Divide mixture between two cake tins, and bake for 25 minutes
   at 180° C (350°F).

Cool on a rack. Remove cakes from tins.

Filling

Beat 2 egg yolks with ½ cup sugar.

Add coffee solution.

Beat chopped butter into mixture.

Add ½ tsp bourbon and stir in remaining ½ cup chestnut purée.

Stir in chocolate pieces.

Cover with cling film and refrigerate.

Topping

Melt chocolate together with 2 tbs cream over low heat.

Stir in 2 tbs bourbon.

Transfer to a bowl, cover with cling film and refrigerate.

Bourbon Chantilly

Whip 2 cups of cream till soft peaks form.
Gradually beat in icing sugar and then fold in 2 tbs bourbon.
Set aside.

Assembly

Spread chilled chestnut filling across top of one cake.
Place second cake on top of first.
Cover assembled cake with chocolate topping and sprinkle with pecan pieces.
Chill for at least 30 minutes.
Serve with Bourbon Chantilly and thrill your family and guests.

CRANACHAN

This traditional Scottish pudding is absolutely delicious and takes only moments to prepare.
Serves: 6

Ingredients:
600ml (1 pint) cream
4 tbs whisky
Quantity runny honey
1 cup oats
2 cups raspberries

Method:
Whip cream until soft peaks form.
Fold through whisky.
Fold in 1–2 tbs honey or more depending on your sweet tooth.
(The recipe works fine without the addition of honey.)

Put cream into individual serving dishes (glass is best, and for a really nice touch, whisky tumblers) and chill.

Dry roast oats in a heavy-based pan, tossing consistently with a wooden spoon until they turn a light golden brown and give off a mild nutty toasted smell.

Remove from heat very promptly at this point so they do not burn.

Remove oats from the pan and set aside.

What you do with the raspberries is a matter of choice.

You can purée them or leave them whole, or purée some and leave the balance in tact, all a matter of taste.

Scatter raspberries or raspberry purée on top of the chilled cream in each individual dish.

Scatter toasted oats on the top of the raspberries and, if wanted, drizzle a little honey across the top of each.

ATHOLL BROSE PUDDING

Adapted from *A Little Scottish Cookbook* by Paul Harris[86] lent to me by Penny Stuart. This is a recipe akin to Cranachan, but without the raspberries. (Although you could of course always add them.)

Serves: 4

Ingredients:
300ml (½ pint) cream
75ml (¼ cup) whisky
3 tsp honey
⅓ cup oatmeal (toasted as above in Cranachan recipe)

Method:
Whip the cream until firm.
Chill for an hour or so, and just before serving, carefully stir through toasted oatmeal and honey, and then the whisky.

Dr. Samuel Johnson famously said, '*Oats, and grain, which in England is generally given to horses … in Scotland supports the people.*' I wonder if he was thinking of whisky at the same time?

Cock of the North, Single Malt Scotch Whisky Liqueur: 'Potential salvation in turbulent times'

This liqueur replicates a recipe dating back to the sixteenth century unearthed at Aboyne Castle by family of my friends Nikki and Jimmy Gordon. It is said that it was a drink given by the 'Cock of the North', the Chief of the Clan Gordon, to his soldiers before they went into, and subsequently won, the Battle of Glenlivet in 1594.

A descendent of his, also Cock of the North, went on to introduce an Act of Parliament that legalised the distilling of whisky in 1823. (See Chapter Nine)

On the bottle today: '*I can well imagine my forebears setting out in defence of their lands with a pewter cask strapped to their sides filled with this precious liquid – potential salvation in turbulent times*'. Signed, Huntly, [the present] Cock of the North

EGGNOG

One of the best party drinks ever. I recall when we made a vast quantity of this one Christmas when I was a child, and there was enough left over to freeze and make into ice cream. The alcohol content slowed down the process but we were tenacious and the eggnog ice cream was one of the best 'leftovers' I have had the pleasure of eating. And eating.

Serves: Up to 16, depending on the size of your eggnog goblets

Ingredients:
4 eggs divided into yolks and whites
½ cup caster sugar and 1 tsp extra
2 cups whole milk
2 cloves
Pinch cinnamon
1 cup cream
1 tsp freshly grated nutmeg
1 tsp vanilla extract
2 tbs bourbon or whisky
2 tbs rum of choice

Method:
Beat egg-yolks until they turn pale.
Slowly add sugar and continue to beat till the mixture becomes creamy.
Set aside.
Combine milk, cloves and cinnamon in a large heavy-based saucepan over medium heat whisking non-stop. Do not let the milk mixture boil.
Remove from the heat and slowly add a small portion of the hot milk to the beaten egg-yolks and sugar, stirring the entire time.
Add combined egg mixture back into the rest of the hot milk and return it to the stove and very gently heat up without boiling. You are seeking only to get to 70°C (160°F) or when the mixture thickens enough to coat the back of a spoon.

Remove from heat, and strain the mixture through a sieve into a large jug.
Stir in the cream and chill for a few hours.
(If the mixture does overheat and parts of it curdle, you can remedy
the problem by running it through a liquidiser, or by beating it with an
electric beater.)
Add nutmeg, vanilla, whisky and rum and return to fridge for an
hour at least.
Whip the egg whites until they form soft peaks; add teaspoon of sugar and
beat a little more.
Fold carefully into the chilled bourbon and rum custard until fully combined.
Serve in chilled cups, or goblets and garnish with a sprinkle of nutmeg.
Brandy balloons are brilliantly suited to serving eggnog.

Cocktails for indulgence[87]
GODFATHER
This is a cocktail to be relied on for a great sense of wellbeing.
Serves: 1

Ingredients:
30ml (1oz) bourbon whiskey
30ml (1oz) Amaretto liqueur
3–4 lumps ice
Slice or two of lime

Method:
Stir the whiskey and Amaretto together in a glass.
Add the ice.
Serve with a slice of lime.

THE HANDSOME MAN

This cocktail is a variation of the Godfather created by my son Harry. He serves it in his bar, The Clubhouse, in Porto Montenegro.

Serves: 1

Ingredients:
30ml (1oz) *Jameson's*
30ml (1oz) Amaretto liqueur
½ an orange
Quantity ice

Method:
Muddle the orange in a shaker.
Add *Jameson's* and Amaretto liqueur.
Add ice and shake vigorously.
Pour into favourite tumbler.

AFTER EIGHT

This may be a little too creamy and rich for some, but worth creating an event just for the experience.

Serves: 1

Ingredients:
30ml (1oz) white crème de cacao
30ml (1oz) white crème de menthe
30ml (1oz) whisky (any style will be fine)
1 small cup espresso coffee
Quantity warm milk to fill

This cocktail has all the pleasure of after-dinner mints, but in a glass. The whisky cuts through the creamy texture to give a good balance to the mix. (Master Sommelier Vincent Gasnier)

Method:
Pour the liqueurs and the whisky into a shaker.
Shake well.
Add the coffee and pour the mixture into a glass.
Stir in warm milk to taste.

ARTILLERY PUNCH

Inspired by *A Guide to Pink Elephants — 200 most requested mixed drinks.*[88] This must date back fifty or sixty years or even as far back as Prohibition. As seen, the combination of ingredients would provide a serious taste sensation not to mention a monumental hangover.
Serves: 30

Ingredients:
1 cup sugar
Juice of 6 lemons
2 tbs Angostura's Bitters
1L (32oz) red wine
1L (32oz) sherry
1L (32oz) rye, bourbon or Scotch
1L (32oz) brandy
1L (32oz) soda or sparkling mineral water

Method:
Mix all ingredients together in a large punch bowl and enjoy the bang!

And on the topic of weaponry…

My friend Cathy not so long accompanied her husband on a business trip to South Korea. There are very clear protocols in place in this ancient of countries and Cathy endured a dinner free of conversation with a certain Mr. Kim as Mr. Kim addressed all his enquiries of Cathy to her husband, and never to her directly. Cathy, like all women, was to be seen but not spoken to.

Anyway, at the conclusion of dinner Cathy's husband, and oddly Cathy too, were invited to a Gentlemen's Club for a little post-prandial refreshment. The establishment was starkly furnished and the group of seven, six bankers, and Cathy, were shown into their own private refreshment room where the only colour was the blue screen on the wall running reels of lewd movies. Then, if their surroundings were not already sufficiently 'other worldly', their host whacked his hand on the table around which they were all seated and demanded of their lady attendant that she bring them all an 'Atom Bomb'.

The Atom Bomb is a cocktail of *Suntory Whisky* placed in a 20ml shot glass fixed inside an elegant schooner, which is then filled to its lips with beer. 'Atom Bomb etiquette' calls for each man present to take his turn and skull the contents of the schooner — whisky and beer — all in one go. The assembled company (Cathy and her husband could only spectate) took it in turns to skull no less than six rounds of Atom Bombs on the trot. Ensuing headaches were predictably pretty explosive.

Chapter 14

Whisky's many identities and interpretations

Whisky, as we know, has a proud position in the phonetic alphabet. When this alphabet was under development in the 1950s no less 31 nations were involved and thousands of comprehension tests run. The aim being naturally to provide 'code' words that would be universally best understood over the airwaves, in essence involuntarily. Whisky is most certainly universally understood.

Whiskey class submarine

This little gem was the first post-war submarine produced by the Soviet navy. The name is unmistakable and not easily forgotten. Would that the whiskey moniker were something to do with whiskey. No, its name's purpose is to be very clear. It is the 'W' class of submarine as opposed to 'V' or 'X'. Its mission like that of its wartime predecessors would have been to locate and destroy enemy warships and merchant shipping. It was considered to be a rather loud submarine. Later it became a very popular export submarine. Three hundred and forty of these boats were originally manufactured and were first launched in 1951. However by 1993 they were extinct.[89]

Whiskey Gap

Whiskey Gap is now a ghost town on what was once a busy commercial thoroughfare between America and Canada. It is located on a pass in the Milk River range on a ridge between the Missouri and Saskatchewan Rivers drainage system. In its heyday in the 1860s and 1870s American traders made their way northwards through it into [what would become] Alberta to trade booze and other goods for buffalo furs. When Prohibition was declared in Alberta in 1916, four years ahead of America, alcohol continued to be successfully smuggled through. That is until America itself became a 'Prohibition nation' in 1920. At this point the flow of alcohol went into full reverse: it was turned about and smuggled straight back south of the border!

Sucking the monkey

What lengths might a sailor go to in order to ease his thirst? And have his *dram o' maut*? He might just find his superiors stashing their prized whisky in small kegs outside their cabin windows, cooling it in the breeze and the shadow of the stern. A nimble sailor would not find it too challenging to position himself strategically, insert a straw, or drinking tube, either into the top of the keg or through a seam, and reward his ingenuity with a long cool draught of whisky, as he 'sucked on the monkey'.

A Whisky of another sort

When you were whisking about doing your errands back in early twentieth century America, you might just have found yourself making use of an open chaise or shay referred to fondly as a 'whisky'. This has prompted me to think about the lyrics to the carol, *Jingle Bells*, and whether they might not originally have been:

> *Dashing through the snow*
> *In a one-horse open shay*
> *Jingle Bells! Jingle Bells!*
> *Oh what fun*
> *It is to ride*
> *In a one-hoss open shay!*

I wonder. It may have been a whisky for Santa, rather than a sleigh all this time...

CONCLUSION AND ACKNOWLEDGEMENTS

A comment on inequitable tax

Australian distillers are at a significant disadvantage on the tax front. Whereas our wine producers, and more recently microbrewers, have certain concessions, that is not the case for the distillers of whisky and other spirits.

A WET tax (Wine Equalisation Tax) is levied on wine producers at 29% (based on the wholesale value of wine) plus GST. However there is a rebate scheme entitling wine producers to a rebate of 29% of the wholesale value of eligible domestic sales *up to a maximum of $500,000* each financial year. Further, the rebate scheme for wine producers applies to *all products* subject to WET, whether they are sold wholesale, retail (at the cellar door, by mail order or internet) or applied to their own use, for example if used for tastings and promotions.

The distillers are not so lucky. They are currently charged a duty of $76.31 per LAL regardless. For the sake of argument therefore, a bottle of whisky at 50% ABV will be charged at 50% of $76.31 being $38.18. (That's per bottle!) Even brandy (what I might consider a close cousin) is let off more lightly being only levied $71.31 per LAL.

Distillers must be eager for any tax incentive. The burgeoning whisky industry is an incredible asset for Australia. The passion being delivered to it by distillers surely will inspire the lawmakers to re-think the maths, and put their support behind the industry which offers a vibrant freshness to an historic practice. The re-emergence of whisky appreciation benefits not only the consumer but also the country at large.

Happily despite all this, there is an abundance of whisky to be enjoyed; a wonderful array of cellar doors and whisky bars at which to explore all manner of malts and blends from all over the world and most importantly I believe I can guarantee that when you order a whisky not only will you have an experience to savour but without fail a conversation will begin ....

Acknowledgements

While writing this book, I have had help from many quarters and consistently I have been shown incredible kinship from members of the larger whisky family. Friends, our children and their friends have lent me books and articles to read, and numerous whiskies to sip. In Hobart Bill Lark and his team have given me much of their precious time, and many invaluable whisky insights; similarly in Victoria David Baker has given me a lot of his time and sound counsel. Here in Sydney, the partners at the World of Whisky have shown me endless kindness and patience in the face of my many — sometimes idiot — questions and uncertainties. The World of Whisky[90] offers a spectacular range of whisky expressions from everywhere in the world, in fact every whisky mentioned in this book so they have been a wonderful resource! Whisky and Alement in Melbourne also offers a vast range of expressions from across the globe.[91] And there is also the Baxter Inn Swillhouse Pty. Ltd. in Sydney to visit for a glass of your favourite whisky or an opportunity to sample something new.

Every aspect of writing about whisky has been thrilling for me. Even when chatting to someone [on the topic] who does not like whisky, a fresh story or opinion has been revealed. The commentary has been endlessly inspiring, and always rewarding. I am so delighted that the idea of writing about whisky popped into my head one day, that my husband thought of the great title,

The Lore of Whisky, and that Jane Curry, my publisher, Cheryl Collins, the book's designer, and Sarah Plant its editor were all on board to give it flight. Thank you everyone.

Sto et stabo!

Endnotes

1   David Daiches, *Scotch Whisky*, Harper Collins, 1969.

2   Kelefa Sanneh, Reinventing a great distillery, http://newyorker.com/reporting/2013/02/11/130211fa_fact_sanneh?currentPage=all (accessed March 2013).

3   Iain Banks, *Raw Spirit*, Arrow Books, 2004.

4   A cratur' is a drinking vessel, from *crater*, the Latin derived from the Greek, derived from the Egyptian, *krater*.

5   Vincent Gasnier, *Drinks*, Dorling Kindersley, 2007.

6   http://archive.org/stream/annalsofkingdomo04ocleuoft#page/784/mode/2up (accessed March 2013).

7   Tom Standage, *A history of the world in six glasses*, Atlantic Books, 2007.

8   Alan Gordon, *The Essential Guide to Scotch* Whisky, E-book.

9   *A Brief History of Scotch Whisky*,(On-line article) http://whisky.com/history.html (accessed March 2013).

10 Dorling Kindersley, *Whisky Opus*, Dorling Kindersley 2012.

11 Jim Murray, world-renowned author of the *Whisky Bible*. Published annually by Dram Good Books Ltd.

12 Britannica Concise *Encyclopedia*.

13 Douglas Fraser, Business and economy editor, BBC News Scotland. 9 January 2013.

14 Ian Buxton, *101 World Whiskies to Try Before You Die*, Hachette Scotland, 2012.

15 Kelefa Sanneh, Reinventing a great distillery, http://newyorker.com/reporting/2013/02/11/130211fa_fact_sanneh?currentPage=all (accessed March 2013).

16 Plain caramel colouring may be added.

17 Iain Banks, *Raw Spirit*, Arrow Books, 2004.

18 Iain Banks, R*aw Spirit*, Arrow Books, 2004.

19 Iain Banks, *Raw Spirit*, Arrow Books, 2004.

20 At Lark Distillery in Tasmania, 1,200 litres of whisky wash at 7.5% ABV is used to produce 400 litres of low wines at 25% ABV, which is redistilled in a spirit run to produce around 120 litres of malt whisky 'spirit heart' at 63.4% ABV.

21 In Australia a copper still may set you back $65,000–70,000.

22 Iain Banks, *Raw Spirit*, Arrow Books, 2004.

23 This stage-two 'liquid' is distilled to between 60% and 72% ABV but critically is then broken down to 63.4% ABV for placement into barrels, the optimum strength at which to do so.

24 Master Blender, Robert Hicks.

25 Kelefa Sanneh, Reinventing a great distillery, http://newyorker.com/reporting/2013/02/11/130211fa_fact_sanneh?currentPage=all (accessed March 2013).

26 British Dictionary.

27 Jim McEwan, distiller at Buichladdich via Kelefa Sanneh, Reinventing a great distillery, http://newyorker.com/reporting/2013/02/11/130211fa_fact_sanneh?currentPage=all (accessed March 2013).

28 John Doxat, *Booth's Handbook of Cocktails & Mixed Drinks*, Pan Books Ltd, 1977.

29 Ian Buxton, *101 World Whiskies to Try Before you Die*, Hachette, 2012.

30 Kelefa Sanneh, Reinventing a great distillery, http://newyorker.com/reporting/2013/02/11/130211fa_fact_sanneh?currentPage=all (accessed March 2013).

31 Ingvar Ronde, *Malt Whisky Yearbook 2012* (7th edn), Magdig Media Limited, 2011.

32 Japanese Whisky, http://japanesewhisky.net/japanese-whiskies.html (accessed March 2013).

33 John Doxat, *Booth's Handbook of Cocktails & Mixed Drinks*, Pan Books Ltd, 1977.

34 This is the leading provider of data on wines and spirits. The IWSR's database is used by all the largest multinational wine and spirits companies as well as many more local companies.

[35] J&B Scotch Whisky, www.whisky.com/brands/jb_brand.html (accessed March 2013).

[36] Kelefa Sanneh, Reinventing a great distillery, http://newyorker.com/reporting/2013/02/11/130211fa_fact_sanneh?currentPage=all (accessed March 2013).

[37] Ingvar Ronde, *Malt Whisky Yearbook 2012* (7th edn), Magdig Media Limited, 2011.

[38] Livingroom Whisky, www.livingroomwhisky.com (accessed March 2013).

[39] Ingvar Ronde, *Malt Whisky Yearbook 2012* (7th edn), Magdig Media Limited, 2011.

[40] Alan Gordon, *The Essential Guide to Scotch Whisky*, E-book.

[41] Alan Gordon, *The Essential Guide to Scotch Whisky*, E-book.

[42] Alan Gordon, *The Essential Guide to Scotch Whisky*, E-book.

[43] Kelefa Sanneh, Reinventing a great distillery, http://newyorker.com/reporting/2013/02/11/130211fa_fact_sanneh?currentPage=all (accessed March 2013).

[44] Alan Gordon, *The Essential Guide to Scotch Whisky*, E-book.

[45] Alan Gordon, *The Essential Guide to Scotch Whisky*, E-book.

[46] Larry Aronson, Director, World of Whisky, Sydney.

[47] Master Blender Robert Hicks quotes, in his words, 'a famous Scotsman'.

[48] World of Whisky, www.worldofwhisky.com.au (accessed March 2013).

[49] The Lark Distillery, www.larkdistillery.com.au (accessed March 2013).

[50] Ian Buxton, *101 World Whiskies to Try Before You Die*, Hachette, 2012.

[51] The Scotch Malt Whisky Society Ltd, The Vaults, 87 Giles Street, Leith, Edinburgh EH6 6BZ.

[52] David Wondrich, Imbibe!, Penguin, 2007.

[53] 'The Irishman Original Clan Irish Whisky', http://alcoholreviews.com/2010/10/28/102010-the-irishman-original-clan-irish-whiskey (accessed March 2013).

[54] Whisky Distilleries in Ireland, http://classicwhiskey.com/distillery.htm (accessed March 2013).

[55] Cheryl Charming, North American Whiskey/Whisky, www.netplaces.com/bartending/whiskey-amber-waves-of-grain/north-american-whiskeywhisky.htm.

[56] Peggy Trowbridge Filippone, About.com Home Cooking, http://homecooking.about.com/bio/Peggy-Trowbridge-Filippone-137.htm (accessed March 2013).

[57] Charles Cowdery, American whiskey connoisseur.

[58] Peggy Trowbidge Fillipone, About.com Home Cooking, http://homecooking.about.com/bio/Peggy-Trowbridge-Filippone-137.htm (accessed March 2013).

[59] John Doxat, *Booth's handbook of Cocktails & Mixed Drinks*, Pan Books Limited 1966.

[60] Mittie Hellmich, *Ultimate Bar Book*, Chronicle Books LLC, 2006.

[61] Alistair Osborne Business Editor, 'Maker's Mark goes a little heavy on the water', The Telegraph. February 11, 2013, www.telegraph.co.uk/finance/newsbysector/retailandconsumer/9863751/Makers-Mark-goes-a-little-heavy-on-the-water.html?fb.

[62] Mittie Hellmich, *Ultimate Bar Book*, Chronicle Books LLC, 2006.

[63] www.omg-facts.com/History/One-Of-The-Reasons-Walgreens-Is-Such-A-L/51571 (accessed March 2013).

[64] 'Hieronymus Brunschwig ou le premier traité imprimé de chirurgie, www.deliciarum.info/29/12/2008/hieronymus-brunschwig-ou-le-premier-traite-imprime-de-chirurgie/ (accessed March 2013).

[65] Lark's Distillery, Tasmania.

[66] Hew Blair, Chairman, Justerini & Brooks Ltd.

[67] Douglas Fraser, Business and economy editor, BBC News Scotland. 9 January, 2013

[68] IWSR.

[69] Hong-Kong based journalist who writes on travel food, drink and culture.

[70] Dorling Kindersley, *Whisky Opus*, a guide to international whiskies, Dorling Kindersley, 2012.

[71] Nicks Wine Merchants, The Lark Distillery, www.nicks.com.au/index.aspx?link_id=76.1612 (accessed March 2013).

[72] In 1839, the Governor of Tasmania, Sir John Franklin, banned 'sly grogging stills' because he saw the young and the restless trapped in a cycle of alcohol-induced chaos.

[73] Nant, Belgrove, Redlands, Mackeys, Tasmania, Old Hobart and McHenrys.

[74] Established in 2004 at Brown Marsh in the central highlands.

[75] There is a micro-distillery industry flourishing in the United States. According to an industry analysis presented at the American Distilling Institute (ADI) Conference in April 2012, there were approximately 50 micro-distilleries operating in 2005; today there are apparently 250 across 45 states and it is estimated that in the 2020s there could be as many as 1,000.

[76] Lark Distillery sources 95% of its barrels from Seppeltsfield Winery in South Australia.

[77] Ingvar Ronde, *Malt Whisky Yearbook 2012* (7th edn), Magdig Media Limited, 2011.

[78] Nicks Wine Merchants, Timboon Railway Shed, http://nicks.com.au/index.aspx?link_id=76.1619 (accessed March 2013).

[79] Ian Buxton, *101 World Whiskies to Try Before You Die*, Hachette Scotland, 2012.

[80] Commonwealth Oil Refineries.

[81] Nicks Wine Merchants, Timboon Railway Shed, http://nicks.com.au/index.aspx?link_id=76.1619 (accessed March 2013).

[82] Similar to a beetroot-come-pumpkin.

[83] Diane Maclean, www.ss-treganna.co.uk/Pdf/SS%20Politician%20PART%20ONE.pdf (accessed March 2013).

[84] Since writing I understand that a further 'limited edition' is under way.

[85] www.matchingfoodandwine.com/news/pairings/20080123/(accessed March 2013).

[86] Paul Harris, *A Little Scottish Cookbook*, Appletree Press, 1988,

[87] Vincent Gasnier, *Drinks*, Dorling Kindersley, 2007.

[88] Richard Rosen Assoc. Inc, A guide to pink elephants, 1952.

[89] History, Development, and Use of the Whiskey Class Submarine, www.russianwarrior.com/1947vehicle_Whiskeyhist.htm (accessed March 2013).

[90] World of Whisky, www.worldofwhisky.com.au (accessed March 2013).

[91] 270 Russell Street, Melbourne, VIC 3000.

INDEX

136

139